Restoring The Soul

Restoring The Soul

Experiencing God's Grace in Times of Crisis

MIRIAM AND STUART BUNDY

MOODY PRESS

CHICAGO

ISBN: 0-8024-6743-1

1 3 5 7 9 10 8 6 4 2

Printed in the United States of America

To
Grace and John Cosby, Jon Bundy, and Valerie Bundy

With appreciation to
Beth Larivee and Christina Tellez for editorial consultation
and to
Aunt Jean, loving caregiver and spiritual counselor

CONTENTS

ACKNOWLEDGMENTS

We are grateful to all those who have prayed for us around the world. We wish to thank the wonderful medical staff at Loma Linda University Physicians Medical Group, Inc.; Miriam's primary physician, Dr. Debra Stottlemyer; surgeon Dr. Brian Fandrich; oncologist Dr. Frank Howard; and oncologist and personal friend Dr. Evert Bruckner. In addition, we thank their gracious and professional support staffs.

To the staff and congregation at Trinity Evangelical Free Church, Redlands, California; the board of trustees of the San Bernardino Community College District; the faculty and staff of both San Bernardino Valley College and Crafton Hills College; the staff and board of trustees of the Moody Bible Institute and the staff of Moody Press, we extend our appreciation.

Though it would be impossible to name all the individuals who have supported us, we wish to name a few in our local community who repeatedly volunteered their leadership in coordinating efforts on our behalf: Elizabeth and Gary Inrig, Cheryl Sells, Carol Frizzell, Beth and Bob Larivee, Marcia Bunnell, Gail Bouslough, Rochelle Baucom, Nancy and Bob Townsend, Skip and Karin Hubby and family, Jack and Nancy Hinkley, Peggy Foskett, and Donna Stark.

Chapter One

SOUL POSSESSION:
Confronting Panic

I'm sorry," the doctor whispered.

Why was a tear slipping from the corner of her eye?

Only later did she tell me how afraid she was for me that day. She knew I might die. I thought only, "We'll cope. This is just an inconvenience."

Since those first numb moments when we were jostled out of the chair of control, our emotions have circled like a musical game, forcing us to flail on the floor or grab onto the seat of faith.

Sometimes the unthinkable and irreversible happens.

When I heard the words *malignant* and *cancer,* I thought of my mother. She had lived thirty years beyond her first occurrence of the disease. I would, too.

But the doctor informed me that this was a rare condition, more difficult to detect. When discovered, it was already considered Stage Three.

I rushed from the hospital to my husband's office.

The diagnosis must have been for someone else, I thought.

We hugged. We couldn't comprehend this change.

Our two older children, Grace and Jon, were home. We decided to tell them immediately. Our youngest, Val, a high school senior, arrived home from school a few hours later.

As a family, we sat together and cried and prayed and decided to go ahead with our plans for the evening, a bridal shower at our house. After all, the bride, Karen, was one of Grace's best friends. Her mother, Nancy, was one of my dear friends. We celebrated with joy and secret, sad silence.

THE CENTRAL ISSUE: SOUL SURVIVAL

The story of our journey that began that day is not about survival of disease. It is about something far more significant. It is the story of the survival of the soul and, specifically, how one can move beyond the pain and permanent scarring of crisis to the restoration of the soul and the creation of new dreams.

I remember those first feelings in the midst of our unexpected, unwanted crisis. I remember waking up and thinking, *This must be a bad dream.*

Sometimes we were buoyed up by a stream of support. At other times we felt the loneliness left over when "advisers" dropped off solutions with the comment, "Don't worry. You'll get over it. I know many people who have."

My daily schedule began to change. I was teaching at the community college, and the medical tests and treatments were interfering with my effectiveness. I had to give up my classes.

I began to feel a dragging, a choking, of my life. I realized it would never be the same. You know inside yourself when normal expectations are hopeless no matter what others say—when awful, disappointing, disruptive events you cannot control cut to the core of your soul.

Every one of us dreams of life working to that pinnacle when we can say, "Ta da! Glory to God!"

As in the tapestry illustration of life, with all the threads someday weaving into a beautiful pattern, I expected a few dark colors. But now the scissors were cutting the cloth of my being. Is this it? Even if I survive death, what can I expect of life?

ATTEMPTING TO CREATE VISION

All of our "somedays" had been loaded onto the hard drive of our lives, and now they were lost in the crash of crisis. Normal, rational thinking became a strain, and our pattern of long-term planning suddenly seemed irrelevant.

We'd based today on goals for tomorrow, tomorrow on goals for the month, this month on goals for the semester, the year, five years, ten years. We'll never forget the fun we had on New Year's Eve many years ago, mapping out future decades of our lives. We made a grid with our names and the names of extended family members on the left-hand side. Across the top, we labeled the years, thirty years in advance. Within the squares, we noted the age that each named person would be throughout the years.

Using this grid, we discussed goals for ourselves and our children. We thought about how we wanted our children to be influenced by their wonderful grandparents and other family members and what that meant in relationship to their ages and planning time together. We considered goals in every realm: social, spiritual, physical, intellectual, cultural, intercultural, financial, educational, musical.

We asked ourselves what we needed to do that year and the next year to meet the goals for five years or ten years. We also discussed how we should grow personally and how we could ready ourselves to be better prepared to help our children with their goals.

Many of those dreams and goals we set in the seventies came true. Now we were approaching the year 2000 and were still thinking twenty, thirty years ahead. It was a terrible blow to even consider that my line on the graph of our lives might end. The doctors were advising us on the survival statistics for my condition for one year and, if we were "lucky" to get past that, the stats for living five years. They did not look good.

[Stuart] I found myself asking what life would be like without this my wife of twenty-five years. How would I cope? My mind went into dizzy scenarios of life situations without Miriam, and I panicked.

Looking backward, I realized again what I had come to realize earlier —that my whole life before marrying Miriam was simply a preamble to the wonderful life that marriage with her has been. She has been my best and closest friend. Together we have learned about life from each other, interacting intellectually and emotionally ever to new heights. She has been my spiritual companion. Together we have shared our faith in

13

Christ, and together we have learned spiritual truths. She has been my trusted confidante.

I thought of past years. While serving as president of Henry Ford College for seventeen years, there were constant pressures on me and on her from unions, faculty senate, student leaders, and community to share confidential information. Never did she break confidence, even though I shared with her the private issues of my job. There were faculty and trustees with whom I would have liked to share confidences, but to do so would have showed favoritism. Miriam became my sounding board on numerous difficult issues such as work stoppages and attempted (but unsuccessful) votes of no confidence. I always felt I would receive an honest, very thoughtful, and confidential response. Often when I faced Detroit's TV news crews during a strike or an angry faculty assembly, I inwardly quaked, but only Miriam knew that, and I could share my inward insecurity with her alone.

I remembered way back to our engagement and the joy of our discovering mutual friends in Mexico and Central America. After our marriage, we enjoyed welcoming students from Guatemala and Costa Rica into our home and serving our church and community together.

I thought of the present and the future, of my job as chancellor with her by my side, of our dreams for reaching out to more lives, for enjoying and encouraging our children and possible grandchildren.

I found my mind wandering. My thoughts tormented me.

[Miriam] Our life, once woven together with the beauty of a carefully stitched garment, lay torn apart like salvaged cloth on a worktable. It was difficult to even imagine what could be made out of the pieces.

We were vulnerable and more emotional. Though we were comforted by expressions of loving support, we wondered if we could continue to live on the edge without a clear view of goals beyond this day.

Moment-by-moment platitudes could not hide the truth in our faces: The meaning of today radically changes without a vision of tomorrow. We had to look beyond and plan for life—not only for death, as some suggested. We considered advice we had sometimes given to others and also listened to counsel in a new light. What did others mean by the phrases they offered? They said: "Get your life in order. Think positively. Be involved in activities. All things work together for good. Enjoy humor. Claim yourself as a survivor."

"GET YOUR LIFE IN ORDER"

One of the most frequent comments we still hear from well-meaning friends is, "Crisis certainly helps you to get your priorities straight."

It is a well-intended but confusing comment. What does it really mean? The assumption must be that our priorities were not straight before this happened, that this disease is a punishment for wrong priorities. Does it follow that, once they are "straight," I will be healed? To us this is a pseudosolution. First, it assumes that you or I have control over or caused our dilemmas, which may or may not be the case. Second, it proposes that a legalistic regime will help us to fix or to feel good about our situation.

Though obviously wrong priorities will hinder both our mental and physical health, we can also feel devastated when following *right* priorities.

Others told me, "Plan your funeral now. Get your last days in order." I was startled. I was praying for life. I was fighting to live.

"THINK POSITIVELY"

Across a wide spectrum of beliefs we hear the advice to think positively. Though we do not dispute the validity of positive versus negative thinking, we believe that this approach also is a vague recommendation.

Positive thinking will not help you regain something you have lost forever. We are not even sure that positive thoughts themselves send healing messages. Perhaps they simply cause us to act in ways that encourage healing. This, like the first proposal, is more a rational response than reality for physical recovery.

It was also difficult, at times, to accept all positive thoughts that overlooked the sadness we felt for this change in our lives. We are grateful to many friends who allowed us to feel grief, especially Gary and Elizabeth Inrig, our pastor and his wife, who had personally experienced a battle with cancer and had showed us the way to begin this journey. They came to the house and shared their shock and comfort and prayers with us the very first day of diagnosis.

"BE INVOLVED IN ACTIVITIES"

"Do not sit home in your bathrobe. Get dressed. Wear makeup."

Good advice. However, as we write this chapter, we are more than a year into this journey, and I am just now accepting the benefit of some hours—some days—sitting at home in my bathrobe. Involvement alone does not reignite the fires for future dreams.

"ALL THINGS WORK TOGETHER"

We believe the Scripture: *"And we know that in all things God works for the good of those who love him, who have been called according to his purpose"* (Romans 8:28).

However, all of you who have faced a crisis of your own will identify with the problem we encountered with the prophets of these "all things" who tried to help by showing us how God brought this trial for good— like a "good" punishment. Resisting defensive feelings, we reminded ourselves to read the Scripture correctly, to remember that He works for our good in all things that He *allows*.

"ENJOY HUMOR"

It was a relief to find things to laugh at. We discovered some movies and television programs that brought temporary distraction. We could appreciate the philosophy of author Norman Cousins, who promoted the idea of "laughter therapy." We believe that humor is a good gift. Humor helps us to release emotion, helps us to connect with our deep feelings and with others. It was, though, merely a relief, not a way to change reality. Laughter does not replace joy.

"CLAIM YOURSELF AS A SURVIVOR"

Throughout this time, we were learning the special language that medicine applies to my situation. The key word is *survivor*. Soon after surgery, my name must have been entered into the "survivor" computer, because now I receive a continual stream of literature for "survivor" events. Technically, I think, one should be considered cancer free to be on that list; but I did survive surgery, and I am still surviving continual treatments of chemotherapy. So I will accept the title.

The survivor syndrome creates a scenario of its own in relation to vision. Are my life dream and my daily data planner dedicated totally to physical survival?

If you are in a different type of crisis, you can probably relate to the urgency of just meeting the daily needs of the one you are helping or of yourself. For you it may be a son or daughter who has chosen another path; a spouse or relative who has betrayed you; a person you loved who died or abandoned you; taking care of dependent adults; living with memories of abuse, harassment, financial loss, or hurtful gossip.

Your pain strains the fibers of your being to focus on survival. In the reality of your life, as in ours, you know that good things such as getting your life in order, thinking positively, involvement in activities, laughter, and even believing that all things work together for good do not lift the fog of sadness that envelops you.

Beyond solving the immediate situation, the most important thing is the survival of the soul. This should not exclude or diminish the importance of focusing on the resolution of my crisis or yours. It should, however, include simultaneous attention to the most important part of your being: the *soul.*

ATTENDING TO THE SOUL

One of the most frequent questions I am asked is, "What matters most?"

Answers often suggested are: love, family, relationships, God.

We already have all of the above. So we ask with the psalmist, "Why are you downcast, O my soul?" (Psalm 42:5).

The question of what matters most must be reformatted to read, What is central to survival and moving beyond? Answers such as those above often appear like inanimate objects that we are grasping to save from a fire. We treasure and feed our connection to these concepts. We savor them like antiques. We see their value. We are fortunate, and we are grateful.

Why is this not enough?

If you are experiencing crisis, you will understand the clear feeling of separation that occurs. Even many "good" things become worthless in view of your situation. They are not bad but irrelevant.

17

My friend Elizabeth says, "You will never see life in the same way again."

The profound truth of her comment resounds again and again as we see each day in a new light.

Even commentaries about love, family, relationships, and God—even these "good" things—can sometimes sound like babble. Why? They fail to connect with my experience. They shove aside the question of my soul.

"Why are you downcast, O my soul?"

How can I move beyond mere survival?

The key must be in answering the question, What is central? What is the core of my being? For no matter how important God or love or relationships are, if they do not connect to my inner self, they become separated, unrelated, irrelevant, and lost in crisis.

The soul—the person within—is the center of our universe and the survival center for faith and dreams. The center is both simple and complex. That is why it is so often disconnected.

The problem we encounter in moving beyond mere physical survival is that we want to touch the soul, but we end up merely poking at separate manifestations of the soul. We can testify how ruthlessly the soul is dissected by many friends and experts. While rightly encouraging my soul to trust God's sovereignty, some ignore or disapprove of my emotions. Others, while focusing on my feelings, will overlook the reality of God's comfort to my soul. And still other friends will clearly indicate that a certain nutritional program alone could prevent or cure both body and soul.

This dissection leaves my inner man knocked down, often bleeding. How can it even survive?

To touch the soul, we must understand that it is more than the sum of parts, a garment of patchwork pieces. The soul is as complete and alive as a whole swatch of cloth. The color of my emotions cannot be separated from the threads of my spiritual yearning or even the hue of physical challenge.

Remember the last time your soul was touched? Would you describe your experience as purely emotional, intellectual, spiritual, physical? It may have been triggered by magnificent music, a stimulating word, a breathtaking view, a private prayer. But what happens in those wonderful, inexplicable moments of epiphany is not limited to a dissected part of you.

You probably would not say, "My soul was touched, but my mind was bored to death." Or, "My emotions were bland, but I was really spiritually energized."

Until we recognize the center of our being as a whole, we cannot move beyond survival to the revival of faith and dreams. This is the view of life that becomes so very clear in crisis. Love, family, relationships, God—all are important to me not as separate objects to be venerated but as I allow them to surround, embrace, and become part of my soul.

A perplexing pattern developed as our family began to walk through this journey.

Though we tried to be open about developments and our feelings, each one of us faced a unique struggle. On my low days, Stuart's spirit was calm. Then, most unpredictably, he would experience anxiety in periods when I felt stronger. Our adult children too, though extremely supportive of us, suffered with our crisis.

One day Grace confided that though she was deeply concerned for me and grateful for the inquiries, "How's your mom?" she noticed that rarely did anyone ask, "How are *you?*"

My immediate family—Stuart, Grace and John, Jon, and Val—were enduring their own private struggle with our crisis.

The soul needs of each one are unique. We are touched by those who reach out to each one of us, to embrace our complete and personal and unique soul.

A PRIVATE PROPOSAL

It is amazing how quickly crisis puts us in a robotic response mode. Our bodies walked through the motions. Our minds were on autopilot. Our emotions were free-flowing. Our souls were not only panicked but often paralyzed.

In trying to do the right thing, our most frequent actions were geared toward maintaining outward normalcy. Stuart went to work, went to church. I would always get dressed, go to church as often as able. Read, cook, respond, accept visitors. This was good and healthy. But this keeping up had nothing to do with the keeping of our souls.

Though we were all trying to support each other as a family, "soul keeping" was one thing that we could not do for each other. Certainly our extension of love and nurture was comforting, but we soon learned that the survival of the soul is a private proposal. We are still learning that we must individually recognize our own souls and take responsibility for the life and growth of our private inner being. We are still learning that it is often easier to ignore the existence of the soul—or to assume that others are responsible for nurturing it. And we are learning that we can begin to confront panic only when we realize that this inner person we possess is uniquely ours and we must choose for it.

EXERCISING THE SOUL

The process of how we are learning to take responsibility for knowing, nurturing, and stretching our souls will be revealed in chapters 2 through 6. This process involves learning to exercise our souls.

We are learning that rarely do we intentionally exercise our souls. No wonder our inner limbs are sore and aching when we must extend them in a crisis. We are definitely still in process. We share our experience with you as we continue to learn. All of our abilities and accomplishments have no power to restore what cancer is taking from us, but we are learning more about a greater power and a more valuable process. As we exercise the soul, we realize the joy of restoring the soul.

Six principles have been evident as we walk through this process. In each chapter we will discuss one of the principles.

The soul exercise principle. As I nourish and strengthen my soul, I am able to revive faith and create new dreams.

Exercising the soul is the process of nourishing and strengthening the center of my being. It is an intentional activity that I prescribe for my inner self. It is a discipline.

Such exercise is private—not in the sense that it must be secret, but it must involve a transformation *within.* Someone else cannot exercise for me. It is not even necessary that anyone else know of this. It is not a matter of achieving something outwardly, then, but allowing an inward work of grace to permeate my soul.

Oswald Chambers writes about a transformation within that is the result of the exercise of God's grace in our souls:

If the Spirit of God has transformed you within, you will exhibit divine characteristics in your life, not just good human characteristics. God's life in us expresses itself as God's life, not a human life trying to be godly. The secret of a Christian's life is that the supernatural becomes natural in him as a result of the grace of God, and the experience of this becomes evident in the practical, everyday details of life, not in times of intimate fellowship with God. And when we come in contact with things that create a confusing and flurry of activity, we find to our own amazement that we have the power to stay wonderfully poised even in the center of it all.[1]

When we choose to exercise our souls, we allow the transformation of grace to limber and strengthen our inner man.

Faith and dreams cannot be revived without attention to the soul. It is the soul that by faith becomes related to God through acknowledgment of His truth and personal surrender to Him. It is the faith conduct inspired by such surrender that seemingly fades in times of crisis and discouragement.[2] We often condemn ourselves or judge others who have "lost faith" in times when the soul seems out of sync with such conduct. To revive our faith, then, we must exercise our soul.

Dreams, too, we discover, are much more than emotional or rational imaginations. Dreams of the future grow deep within the soul in intangible ways that often defy analysis. To revive our dreams too, we must exercise the soul.

The process of moving beyond emotions to faith and dreams is a journey of grace full of joyous moments. As we began this journey, we continually asked ourselves, "What does faith mean at a time like this?"

Perhaps more difficult has been coming to a meaningful answer. How does faith make our lives, emotions, minds, or physical health any different at this moment of suffering from someone's without faith? Our heads knew all the given answers, but we wanted what was real and worked in the middle of panic.

This book explores the process of how faith works to revive our souls and help us soar beyond survival to the re-creation of dreams.

Though interest in the soul is popular in our culture today, we realize that understanding it is not simple. Philosophers and theologians have debated its definition throughout the ages. Not as authorities, but in respect for what others have concluded about the soul, we shall consider the meaning of the soul in the Appendix of this book.

The following principles will be further developed as they relate to the story of our journey:

Chapter 2: As I focus on positive and praiseworthy passions, I am able to confront fear and experience peace.

Chapter 3: As I acknowledge the complexity of my soul, I learn to overcome anxiety and accept love.

Chapter 4: As I extend my soul through intercession for others, I am able to move beyond impatience and experience joy.

Chapter 5: As I release my soul to God and enter into His presence, I am able to trust and experience faithfulness and gentleness.

Chapter 6: As I cling to the Source of soul power, I am able to regain vision and hope.

Then, in chapter 7, we will address the mysteries of soul connection —connecting with people and with God.

Each principle and the exercise it involves acknowledge the importance of nurturing, stretching—possessing our souls. With that acceptance we will not only confront panic but will move beyond survival to the realization of faith and dreams.

We can testify that the results of these exercises are greater far than you can imagine. By following them, you will open the door to experiencing the true benefits of spiritual growth: love, joy, peace, patience, kindness, goodness, faithfulness, gentleness, and self-control (Galatians 5:22–23).

Each exercise will encourage you to take a step forward. Soul passion leads you to the secret of peace. Soul confirmation allows you to find the opportunity to love. Soul intercession will guide you to the path of patience and goodness. Soul restoration encourages faithfulness and gentleness, and soul connection reveals the source of joy.

CHOOSING TO MOVE BEYOND SURVIVAL

When we decide to exercise our soul, we inevitably involve the mind. It is popular to talk about spirituality today as part of a mind exercise. The Bible speaks of the Spirit, received by those who come to God through His Son:

But when the time had fully come, God sent his Son, born of a woman, born under law,

to redeem those under law, that we might receive the full rights of sons.

Because you are sons, God sent the Spirit of his Son into our hearts, the Spirit who calls out, "Abba, Father." (Galatians 4:4–6)

The Bible further states: "Since we live by the Spirit, let us keep in step with the Spirit" (Galatians 5:25).

Can we exercise the soul without exercising the spirit? Can we be spiritually exercised without the Spirit of God?

Chapter Two

SOUL PASSION:
Confronting Fear

---

*Y*ou look so good," people would say.

I was numb and unable to assess *how* I looked or felt. Even my family did not realize how the shock of this crisis had anesthetized me. But when waves of fear shook my soul from slumber, I began to feel the pain of exposure to the frostbite of life. Fear is like that—like a freeze that creates icicles. Fear hardens our emotions into daggers that threaten to slash the soul.

I began to experience the cold reality of this truth during the first weeks of testing and chemotherapy. My many medical appointments, mixed with holiday celebrations, pushed me into a surreal world of numb response to the flow of events.

EVENTS SCATTER THE SOUL

I did not want to feel fear. I would cry alone and dry my tears in order to be strong for the family. After all, Thanksgiving and Christmas were coming.

We were both captivated and sobered by the great events and announcements of the season. We especially celebrated the engagement of Beth and Bob. Beth, my first cousin, though closer in age to my daughter, is a dear and treasured friend. Both she and Bob are a joy to our entire family. The exciting news of their engagement came the day after we first learned of my cancer. The timing was like good medicine to the soul.

We love to celebrate with family and friends, and that Thanksgiving was no exception. Three generous sisters—Casey, Mary, and Michelle—swooped in with table decorations and food for our entire dinner. Our guests included extended family and friends from our church and from others as far away as Guatemala.

We declared our thanksgiving with the psalmist: "Those who trust in the Lord are like Mount Zion, which cannot be shaken but endures forever. As the mountains surround Jerusalem, so the Lord surrounds his people both now and forevermore" (Psalm 125:1–2).

We read this with our guests, feeling new meaning and appreciation.

There were eleven of us altogether, and the fun and fellowship of the day cheered our souls. Friends of a lifetime, Carlos and Sonja, with sons Daniel and Jose, came all the way from Guatemala. Carey, a childhood friend and recent reacquaintance, joined in the fun by requesting everyone to wear a "turkey" (silly) tie. Our friends from church, Craig and Mary Ellen, with daughters Julia, Claire, and Hannah, shared our table as well.

However, the highs of the holidays and the physical lows induced by chemotherapy began to scatter our souls. Everything that occurred each day, both good and bad, deeply touched our emotions. Our deepest fears were allayed only temporarily by the warmth and celebration of the season.

SUPPORT SURGES AND PROTECTS

We celebrated Christmas with a deep sense of gratitude for the meaning of Christ's birth and the life He has given to us.

The surge of support from friends and family was overwhelming. I remember thinking, *I never could have imagined that so many people cared.*

There had been times during earlier months of that year that I felt so alone, especially when caring for my elderly father. Now our church family, especially the women's ministry and our small Bible study group, provided food and assurance of their prayers many times a week. Those far away called and sent cards. I kept every card from both near and far and continued to look forward to them. They represent people who really care and want me to live.

I thought of my friends in past years who had been ill. I had bought cards and written letters, but I had never realized how much they would mean to me in the same situation. They were like infusions of life into my soul.

STRESS STRIKES THE SOUL

As we moved into the new year, my strength began to wane. My hair fell out, and I experienced the effects of my blood count's dropping, which caused tiredness and required isolation from crowds. This isolation was and still is one of the most difficult adjustments for me. I missed the interaction with students, since I was no longer teaching. I missed the independence of driving. It was not that I was prohibited from driving or seeing people, but very often I did not feel up to it. And, of course, when my blood count was low, I was at risk of exposure to germs.

Stress began to fray my soul.

PHYSICAL LASHES

I was whipped with questions about the changes in my body.

What if I have this chemo-caused burning, numbing, vacant lack of feeling sensation forever? What if I don't get better?

I felt like a helpless slave to cancer and chemotherapy, with no rights, no way out, no promise of freedom. It was difficult to accept physical pain and weakness.

"Remind me," I would say to Stuart, "why would I want these nauseating treatments? Why am I doing this? Oh, yes, remind me. I do want to live!"

SOUL BEATING

Everything I heard and every thought I had stayed with me. I replayed each word offered in my behalf and beat myself with conclusions about my weakness.

In addition, the physical stress on my body and emotional stress of the unknowns began to color my concept of soul and faith.

Gray clouds of fear and depression often threatened to engulf me like the morning fog. Rather than staying in bed, I would waken early, compelled to get up and get dressed. I was determined not to stay under the covers of this fog. I would not let this beat me! Still the questions came. I wanted to be honest and really think about them.

DOES FAITH HAVE FEELINGS?

I wanted to "feel" that God would heal me. Shouldn't I feel that way if I had enough faith? My lack of feeling jostled me between two strong-armed figures: Doubt and Denial. If I didn't "feel" that I would be healed, was I doubting God's power? On the other hand, if I did "feel" I would be healed, was I merely denying reality?

I carefully weighed people's comments. "It is God's will that you be healed," some would say.

I prayed for healing. But I remembered friends who had also prayed that prayer, and they died. Was I willing to accept that possibility?

DOES FAITH LIVE IN THE FUTURE?

"Just think—you will be with your loved ones and Jesus in heaven," a few would cheerfully remind me.

At first it was difficult to explain why I did not feel their delight in the thought of death. I was confused. I was torn. To be in the presence of the Lord would be glorious. Therefore, my fears were and are not of death itself. I know with absolute certainty that I will spend eternity in heaven because of God's gift of eternal life through Jesus Christ.

No, it was not death that I feared, but the death of dreams. I wanted to see my children grown, independent, married, with children of their own. I wanted to share this with Stuart. These desired images seemed to shatter in my face and cut to the core of my soul.

If I die, the dreams we share will die for me. They will be shared with others, I thought.

Even though I do not "feel" faith, I know it has not been snatched from me. I do believe. I know faith is not only for assurance of the future, but how does it help me with the fear that I feel today as I grieve my lost tomorrows? I pondered this.

The question persisted. How could I confront fear and experience peace?

DOES FAITH MEAN FATALISM?

I was amazed at how many people said to me, in a sincere attempt to empathize, "None of us has a guarantee. I could be hit by a car and die today."

That is true, but it was difficult for me to be comforted by this. I had difficulty separating this response from the fatalistic philosophy "Whatever will be will be." Where does my soul fit in here? Does my soul's communion with God make no difference? Fatalism, in my mind, eliminates hope and the existence of divine possibilities.

I was troubled by the equating of emotions in the "I could die too" comments. I wondered, *Should my emotions be so easily dismissed?*

Though any one of us could die when crossing the road, we continue to program our lives, shop, and relate to others with a view to years ahead. Suddenly, the uncertainty of my own life aroused every emotion within me. *I could not plan and react in the same way.*

DOES FAITH ELIMINATE FEAR?

Fear of depending. It was not only fear of a shortened life but the prospect of living with disease that frightened me. Would I be in pain and discomfort for the rest of my life on this earth? Would I become dependent, disfigured?

We were still mourning the recent loss of three dependent adults—my father, Stuart's sister Nancy, and Aunt Harriet. I remembered with sadness their difficulties. Even if I survived, it was depressing to think that I too might be prematurely old and dependent on others.

Fear of anonymity. I remember my dear godly father mumbling one day about not wanting to be treated like a piece of furniture.

"What?" I asked.

"I don't want to be treated like a piece of furniture," he repeated. "You know. When someone tells you to sit in this chair and be comfortable, then moves you to another chair and leaves you there. That is what they do to old people."

29

Now I began to understand and fear that I too would be treated like an inanimate object, moved about or settled as others think I should be.

Fear of labels. In the first few weeks and months we were inundated with books and clippings about cancer. We read them all, eager to be well-informed about what was happening. But another fear grew out of this. Were the threads of my relationships deep and bonding to my soul or merely loosely basted on the surface to the woman with cancer?

I was uncomfortable carrying the banner of cancer as my identity. I did not want to become synonymous with cancer. That was and still is a discipline, often failing my effort to go beyond the disease and work on growing relationships.

Fear of statistics. Stuart experienced the lash of fear when hearing from our surgeon the statistical probabilities for life and death.

[Stuart] While Miriam was undergoing surgery, I gathered with dear friends in the waiting room to hear the results. Finally, after what seemed an interminable wait, the surgeon appeared.

He informed us that the operation was a success. However, he frankly predicted that Miriam would die.

We stood in stunned silence.

Finally, half stammering, I asked, "She will die? What is your prognosis?"

He told us that she had a very aggressive form of cancer, which would result in her death.

"As to a time frame?" I asked apprehensively.

He explained the statistical probabilities—possibly five years, maybe ten.

We stood looking at each other, staggered. The news was shattering. We needed to know, but it was painful, arousing such distress that we at first felt anger.

"How can he say such a thing?" we grumbled.

Later, our friend Ralph Winter, chancellor of William Carey University in Pasadena, would give me this picture of death:

"Imagine death as a lion," he said. "We hear him roaring through the

30

forests of life, and sometimes in the death of a friend we see his shadow. Then one day the leaves part, and the lion of death steps out of the forest, and we see his face for the first time. Life is never the same after that encounter."

On that day in the waiting room, the lion of death appeared, and life has never been the same. Death has become more to be considered than ever before.

EXERCISING SOUL PASSION

[Miriam] We were both learning that fears can cause faith and dreams to fade. How could we confront those fears and discover peace? We began to learn in those early weeks that there is an exercise of the soul that melts fear and brings the warmth of peace back into our lives. It is an exercise that must be repeated over and over again, for in the ensuing weeks and months we found fear lurking around the corner many times, blowing its chill into our souls.

[Stuart] After seeing the lion of death face to face, does that mean life should forevermore be dreary, apprehensively awaiting the end? Not so. Not so for a number of compelling reasons. For one, this knowledge places all of life in sharp focus, so that the things that truly matter become more important and those that matter less begin to fade in importance.

The sanctity of life becomes preeminent. When Miriam laments the effect of the mastectomy and the chemotherapy on her appearance, I am able to remind her that it was her soul, her life, that I fell in love with. And so as I focus on her precious soul, I see beyond the scars of her treatment, and I see the special, wonderful person I fell in love with and love even more today.

[Miriam] Stuart began to focus automatically on what was most important to him. While aware of the negative implications of our circumstances, he shifted his thoughts to the positive value of our relationship.

My own awareness of a change of focus was slower and came about a different way. As we shared our changing emotions with each other, neither Stuart nor I—though shocked and perplexed—sensed an urging to flee from our faith. Nevertheless, we admit that our feelings were certainly blurred by the overwhelming weight of what is known as the Big C—cancer.

One day I was concentrating on Scripture, looking for verses that would help me respond to the Big C. "What does God say about healing? How do I respond in suffering?" I asked myself. I felt that I was suffocating under the weight of the Big C.

Then, suddenly, it was clear that my focus had been centered on the wrong C. I had let the cold pressure of fear establish *cancer* as the Big C, the controlling element in my daily existence.

I saw the words of the apostle Paul: "I have been crucified with Christ and I no longer live, but Christ lives in me. The life I live in the body, I live by faith in the Son of God, who loved me and gave himself for me" (Galatians 2:20).

"The Big C in my life is *not* cancer; it is *Christ!* He is greater than cancer. *He* controls my life, not cancer," I announced to myself.

And then it became clear. It is not my faith *feelings* that must be strong, but my faith focus that must remain strong.

As I thought more about focus, I realized that it is directly tied to the principle of soul passion. Far beyond an exercise of positive visualization, it is an experience of transformation.

Soul passion principle: As I focus on positive and praiseworthy passions, I am able to confront fear and experience peace.

What is a soul passion exercise?

Soul passion exercise involves the shifting of focus away from self to positive and praiseworthy interests. The activities on which I choose to focus will benefit my soul if they are deliberately selected for their positive value, if they are compatible with my interests and abilities, and if they are consistently followed. Coming to understand the importance of deliberate selection, a compatible selection, and a consistent selection of praiseworthy interests is the key to the soul passion exercise.

MAKE A DELIBERATE SELECTION

In making a deliberate selection, we turn from self-centered passions to the cultivation of activities of positive value. The soul passion exercise involves deliberately choosing a habitual activity of eternal value to the soul. The soul passion exercise involves the wholehearted and persistent cultivation of a distinct area of thought or activity that enlightens and enlivens my soul.

But I have no energy for this, I thought.

Then I realized that all this exercise requires is for me to use the same amount of energy that I am already giving to fear and allocating it to focus for the good of my soul. I was concentrating all of my energy on the Big C and all the negative consequences of this disease. When I began to reallocate my energies to focus on a positive passion, I discovered the first step of this soul exercise.

How can I do this?

When I am full of fear, I will think about spiritual things, I began.

That was good, but it was not an exercise of passion. My thoughts would wander, and my body and emotions distracted me from the process. I needed to single out a specific area of thought or activity and passionately pursue it.

It was actually a gift from our cousins Mary and Bob that helped me begin a soul passion exercise without realizing it. During those first months, they sent us a beautifully framed drawing and a book. The drawing was of Jesus as the Lamb of God, comforting a small sheep. It is a portrait that touches the emotional part of my soul for it illustrates the compassion of Christ. The book that Mary and Bob sent was *Trusting God,* by Jerry Bridges. It is a wonderful study of the sovereignty of God.

These two gifts inspired me to study the attributes and character of God. As I created a notebook and began to see more clearly the truth of who God is, I found that my passion for knowledge and understanding of truth brought about a change. As I searched for illustrations and understood more of God's character, I was able to confront fear.

For example, I studied the many ways in which God demonstrated His love and faithfulness to His people Israel. I was reminded of how everlasting is His love, how unending His faithfulness. And this same God offers His love and faithfulness to me in my circumstances. Now I confronted fear with knowledge and experience, with the Person who is loving and faithful, and peace began to invade my soul.

By choosing a specific area on which to focus—the attributes of God—and devoting repeated thought and energy to growth, knowledge, and understanding in this area, I was exercising soul passion. When I exercised soul passion, I discovered excellent and praiseworthy knowledge and truth, and the truth began to lift me from fear and despair to energy and love.

I can study truth, look for truth, honor truth in all areas of life, not only in the area of theological study. I can investigate truth in history, science, and nature. It widens my perspective and lifts my soul away from fear.

This deliberate selection of focus is the first step to a soul passion exercise. In the process, I chose to continue pursuing the gifts and interests of my soul. Often in crisis we are tempted to stop everything we are doing, thinking we have no time for anything other than crisis management. However, we can make a choice to still think about and pursue our interests. As much as possible, we need to keep on doing what we are called to do.

MAKE A COMPATIBLE SELECTION

With this in mind I began to ask myself anew, "What is my purpose? What can I pursue with passion now, with my limitations?"

As I remembered family members who faced difficult circumstances, I realized that there are many different ways to exercise our soul passions. Each soul is complex and unique, each thriving as it pursues what is true, noble, right, pure, lovely, and admirable in a variety of areas. Our individual gifts, our interests, our purpose in life—how we are designed—determine our passions.

Aunt Harriet was a caregiver to her niece Nancy for many years, even to the age of eighty. We often marveled at her continuing cheerful spirit and energy. Though she carried an enormous burden, her soul thrived. She had a gift for music and art, which she nurtured throughout the disrupting responsibilities she carried. She was designed with the soul of an artist and musician. She followed that design by creating beautiful oil paintings and using her skill on the piano and marimba, always seeking excellence and giving praise to God. I saw and heard her fears at times, but I also saw how she confronted them and was able to embrace peace.

Another aunt comes to mind, Aunt Grace. She not only lost a husband just nine months after their marriage, but she cared for an invalid father, ran a business, and took care of children in her home as a young widow. All who knew her would agree that she was one of the most delightful and inspiring people that they knew. Her passion was people, and she continued to encourage and care for others all of her life. She confronted her fears with persistent dedication to those in her care so that all around her were continually blessed by her warm and peaceful spirit.

A third example is my mother, Valerie, whose soul continued to soar as cancer dissipated her body. Her creative passions were exhibited even in her last days. She reminded us that she was getting ready for a party. She was referring to a celebration in heaven. Her deep love of people brought many to her bedside. She reached out to each one, asking about each need and activity. She was still able to bring people together creatively and praise God through it all. She loved music, although she could no longer play the violin. She encouraged those who visited her to sing. She was so filled with peace in those last days that her countenance glowed and she appeared as a young girl, though she was seventy-five. She had been transformed.

These women showed me that each person's designed interest must be followed. As I continue to use my gifts and praise God, He will transform my soul and lighten my spirit.

MAKE A CONSISTENT SELECTION

In addition to making a deliberate selection and a compatible selection, a consistent selection is vital to the effectiveness of soul passion. Filling time with one activity after another without consistent devotion to a specific and praiseworthy focus, causes me to ignore both confrontation with fear and the need for growth in my soul. To face my fear and fill my soul, I must continue on in the development of my gifts day after day, even if just a little bit. As I focus on the positive—the pure, true, lovely, and noble—my soul is revived. It may not seem so at first, but it is the beginning of a process that will allow us to grow and create new dreams.

PRACTICAL EXERCISES FOR BEGINNING

Though the soul passion exercise is similar on the surface to positive thinking techniques, it moves me beyond mere survival by the unique way it involves my soul. First, positive thinking can be accomplished by simple discipline of the mind, but, to be effective, soul passion exercise requires the activation of my whole being. Second, whereas positive thinking is often related to self-affirmation, a soul passion exercise always involves the recognition of excellence and praise outside of the self.

The following are four practical ways by which I began to exercise soul passion in those early months. At first, these exercises may appear to be very simple. However, even the most basic activities can seem impossible to a person in crisis. Therefore, it is important to encourage one idea at a time, consistently cultivating it until it becomes a part of your routine, which ultimately nourishes the soul.

The activities that I began with were creating Scripture Cards, designing a Blessing Box, beginning a Character Study Notebook, and gathering Listening Clues.

Scripture Cards. Those who have gone through chemotherapy know that there are periods of time when one has absolutely no energy or even the desire to read. I certainly experienced that. Some days I felt as if I could not even lift my Bible. But I spent many hours sitting at the doctor's office and the hospital, waiting for tests and treatment, and it was often boring. I tried carrying my Bible and books. But when I was fatigued, they were often too heavy and cumbersome. And then I wouldn't feel up to reading.

What helped me through those days were Scripture Cards. On good days, I would write down Scriptures of praise on three-by-five cards. I would slip a bundle of these into my purse and focus on them while waiting for various treatments. The advantage was that I could carry them anywhere. They were easy to access and then to put away when the nurse called.

These verses were, and still are, a source of tremendous blessing to my soul. Writing them down gave me the incentive to pursue my thinking and review of them day after day. Soon my friends began to give me specific verses of encouragement, and my pack of Scripture Cards expanded. Every day I passionately searched for new understanding of these verses. This activity of focusing on Scripture meditation helped me to look away from myself and look upward to God.

Blessing Box. A second exercise that helped me shift away from myself to consistently and specifically practice praise and thanksgiving was the creation of a Blessing Box. As cards and letters poured into our mailbox, I was overwhelmed with the love and goodness of so many, many friends. I realized that I was truly blessed, and I began reviewing their cards week after week with gratitude. I saved them in a box, which I called my Blessing Box. Soon my big box was overflowing, and I needed a second. When that one was filled, I reorganized them in a file.

Today, after more than a year of treatment, I am never without the reminder of those who still pray and care. All I have to do is get out my Blessing Box file and thank God for each one who took time to write. The Blessing Box exercise has helped me to be more specific in expressing my gratitude.

A passionate focus on gratitude changes your perspective. Oprah Winfrey has encouraged millions in her viewing audience to keep what she calls Gratitude Journals. The idea is to write down five things for which you are grateful each day. It certainly fits as a soul passion exercise, as one must be focused and persistent to continue it. Taking such a list and using it as a basis for a prayer of thanksgiving to God would be an excellent and praiseworthy exercise.

Character Study Notebook. My third soul passion exercise involves the discipline of studying the character of God. It is ongoing as I seek to understand, first through Scripture and then through life examples, the consistency and wonder of God's character. It helps me to write down my observations, so I created a little notebook for myself. I started with notes from a Bible scholar and am building on that. As I correctly understand God's character, I am able to focus on what is true, and His truth brings peace to my soul.

Listening Clues. Those of us in crisis hear things we have never heard before. Words of comfort and advice take on new meaning. Perhaps they are the very words we have said to others, but in our own crisis we hear them differently. Some words are full of meaning, others confusing, and still others blatantly offensive on the surface. What my dear husband helped me realize was that *all* words are intended to encourage and comfort and those speaking them often feel awkward and helpless.

I began to listen more intently. I listened with appreciation. It is so easy when one is ill to focus on the self. As I learned to shift my focus to others, I was able to hear the needs and joys in their lives. I learned more about them than I had ever imagined.

By listening to the voices of others, and listening to the voice of God, we are able to challenge our fears and change our focus.

Both Stuart and I are learning that by shifting our focus from self and devoting spiritual energy to what is positive and praiseworthy, we exercise soul passion and experience peace.

CHOOSING TO MOVE BEYOND SURVIVAL

In times of crisis, it seems that our usual passions are severed from our souls. How can we pursue something that is no longer there, that is no longer possible? Not only do we ask, What is the purpose of this? but we ask, What is my purpose now? This is my greatest fear: that my life has no purpose now.

Is this because my *plans* are no longer possible? I need to move beyond plans to purpose. There is a proverb that says, "Many are the plans in a man's heart, but it is the Lord's purpose that prevails" (Proverbs 19:21).

Does a change in my plans change His purpose for my life? Even though I see the unraveling of my plans as a bad experience, will God's good purpose for my life still be fulfilled?

SUMMARY

My goal in this exercise is to shift my focus from self and negative thinking to positive and praiseworthy interests. I am motivated by the need to confront fear with truth. Therefore I actively pursue what is true, noble, right, pure, lovely, and admirable in my specific areas of interest. Practical suggestions include establishing a method for focusing on Scripture meditation, creating a Blessing Box, studying the character of God, and practicing attentive listening. The benefits of this exercise are that my fears begin to fade and the peace of God embraces my soul.

Chapter Three

SOUL CONFIRMATION:
Confronting Anxiety

I have a remedy that a friend told me about," the person would begin.

People were eager to help us, and every leaflet, fax, internet memo, or book loaned to us suggested new possibilities. We wanted to learn all we could about this disease and not succumb to ignorance.

When I did not feel like reading more cancer stories, Stuart was always ready to keep track of the research. He really did it all, digesting and comparing traditional, alternative, and natural nutritional remedies. We never imagined the reams of material that would involve.

Our first information came from our doctors in the form of booklets and information sheets. The doctors were very thorough, always following explanations with written material. We watched, listened, and felt complete confidence in their expertise.

At the same time, alternative solutions were presented to us, and we were curious and open to learn of these as backup solutions. Sometimes we were astounded by the extreme measures offered. Would these friends really try that if *they* had cancer? Sometimes we felt uncomfortable pressure, as if our friendship depended on our allegiance to their advice.

THE OVERLOAD OF "SIMPLE" SOLUTIONS

Compelling personal testimonies of solutions that worked for others could not be completely ignored. At the same time, advocates beat the warning drums of death—do, do, do this or die. We were overloaded with options. Even in our vulnerable emotional state, we knew that no one could benefit from *all* of these alternatives; yet each implied that to ignore it was to choose death.

My mind and emotions were overloaded, unable to accommodate all of this. Instead of offering hope, each new solution proposed began to produce anxiety. It was indeed better for Stuart to take over the analysis of all the materials.

[Stuart] As news of Miriam's cancer reached our friends near and far, we began to receive recommendations from them about a wide range of alternative solutions and traditional cancer treatments. These friends were eager to help us and wanted to show their concern by offering some treatment they could recommend.

Simply forget it. One friend suggested that the traditional treatment approach actually did more harm than good. It might be better to forget altogether the suggested protocol of surgery, radiation, and chemotherapy —Cut! Burn! Poison!

We received some literature propounding this view. The argument was that these are three "approved" paths to the graveyard! It suggested that surgery only mutilates, cannot remove the cause of the cancer, and possibly even hastens its spread. Radiation, the "burn," destroys healthy cells and weakens resistance. And chemotherapy, the "poison," is but part of a multibillion dollar death mill that cannot cure.

Simply eat this. There was no question that Miriam's surgery was disfiguring. Was it really necessary? It was not pleasant to look forward to the chemotherapy and radiation, with their serious side effects. For a moment it was easy to believe that shark cartilage or apricot pits would be easier on her and perhaps just as effective.

As I watched the effects of the traditional treatments, Miriam's overwhelming weakness, her loss of hair, her despondency at her inability to function normally, her insecurity with her changed appearance, I could not help but ask, "May not these alternative treatments be a kinder, more effective way?"

Simply supplement. The writings of Linus Pauling were sent to us. He wrote that massive doses of vitamin C were effective in preventing and in curing cancer. The paper failed to mention that both Pauling and his wife died of cancer after lengthy massive doses of vitamin C.

Other supplements were suggested, such as special vitamins available through mail-order companies.

Simply shape up! One popular book suggested that tension and anxiety brought on cancer—that, as a result, the cancer Miriam was suffering was her own fault and that if she wanted to be cured she needed to take coffee enemas.

What to believe? I desperately wanted the best for Miriam, to see her free of cancer and free of the side effects of the traditional methods of poison, slash, and burn. Did we dare abandon our good doctors at the famed Loma Linda Hospital, and later at the City of Hope, and embark on a program of alternative medicine on our own, whether laetrile, or shark cartilage, or vitamin C?

I attended a seminar on cancer quackery to get a better sense of what was available. The seminar, attended by some five hundred genuinely concerned elderly people, was interrupted by a representative from a New Orleans clinic, who tried to take over the seminar with a presentation about "antineoplastons."

With information about these conflicting treatments whirling around in my head, I felt very much alone. How could so many godly people have such differing views? What counsel could I give my beloved Miriam that would be best for her at this critical time in her life?

Counsel with Dr. Evert Bruckner, a dear medical doctor in our church who specializes in oncology, was helpful. He reminded me that alternative methods unsubstantiated by the Institutes of Cancer Research were still a risk and that traditional treatments are constantly being im-

41

proved and shown to be more helpful. "They are the best we have today," he assured me.

He further explained that as alternative methods are tested with the same rigors as traditional treatments, we will see some becoming part of traditional treatment.

We needed to make a decision, and we decided to stay with the Loma Linda Hospital and, later, with the City of Hope. We felt confidence in the cancer specialists we had come to know and trust, yet we continued to read with interest all that continually came to us on alternative treatments.

STRUGGLING WITH ANXIETY

[Miriam] In contrast to the fears I had experienced, fears based on the facts of my condition and the reality of my experience, I think it is important to explain the different kind of difficulty I had when dealing with anxiety. At first I equated anxiety with fear and tried to deal with it in the same way. Anxiety is different though, more illusive, without a face. I tried to bury it and realized that was denial.

It was February, three months into chemotherapy, and I was used to the unpleasant physical side effects of the treatment. It was easy to attribute any down feeling to nausea, the constant metallic taste, and lack of energy. I steeled myself. I thought, *I will be all right.*

Surgery was scheduled for April. I thought, *I can handle the surgery. After all, my mother did. I never heard her complain.*

Though I recognized that surges of anxiety would occasionally rush through me, I was hesitant to confess these feelings to others. I continued to rationalize, believing I could scare away anxiety with sensibility.

Nevertheless, anxiety kept returning, slipping secretly in and out through the cracks in my soul like little whips of wind. In quiet moments of sleepless nights, I thought about the possibility of not surviving. It was dreadfully painful, difficult to think about, and impossible to talk about.

SEPARATION ANXIETY

My soul was not suffering from an anticipation of homelessness at the point of death. It was a different kind of pain, a sensation that I knew in a small measure as a mother. It was the anxiety a mother feels the first day her child leaves for school or—even worse—when she loses a child. It was separation anxiety.

Compounded many times over was the sense of dread I felt at the thought of separation from my wonderful husband and dear children. It was unbearable to think of not being with them or them with me. Separation anxiety makes one feel alone even when with others. It is more than the pain of isolation from a physical presence. It is the pain of alienation of the soul.

IMAGINATION ANXIETY

I imagined my husband distraught and grieving. I imagined his coming home to an empty house. I knew he would not like that. I imagined his looking for things that I usually find. I saw him crying—something he never does. I agonized in my mind. I would be the cause of this.

Then I thought of my children—though grown and competent—hurt and maybe angry, lonely in their grief. I didn't want to cause them this terrible pain. My anxiety for my family grew.

MATURATION ANXIETY

Another thought troubled me. Maybe no one would pray for my family every day. Who else but parents pray many times a day forever for the maturing lives of their children? Who else but a husband or wife prays for the other many times a day forever? Who would pray for my husband? Who would pray for my children? I see—now—how great God is in providing dear loving friends to take up the banner of prayer for the continued maturation and growth of my family. However, during those first months of illness, I was continually plagued by anxiety about their future.

LEARNING TO UNLOAD AND LIGHTEN THE SOUL

It was difficult to see the big picture of what was happening to my soul. Anxiety kept interfering with my perspective. One day when I was talking with my cousin Beth, a very wise young woman, I realized that I was telling her about some of these anxieties, and she encouraged my confession as a healthy process. These thoughts had been hovering in my soul and weighing me down. To acknowledge that they were part of my being was a great relief.

At the same time, my friend Carol visited me and made similar observations about the value of acknowledging the complexity of our thoughts and emotions. She noted that I was experiencing a process similar to grieving a death. In a strange way, I was grieving the loss of physical health and even the possibility of death much as others would experience the stages of grief in the death of a loved one.

As I experienced a mixture of guilt, anxiety, and depression over this, I remember Peggy's listening and understanding right where I was. We were eating together at Kay's Cafe. Her quiet counsel opened the way for me to admit my true feelings and struggles. Her acceptance of my feelings freed me to be more direct when other friends asked how to pray for my specific needs.

I shared some of my thoughts with those who kept me in their daily prayers. As I began to feel more freedom to express my feelings with these friends who live close around me, I was relieved that they did not seem shocked or reproving. I began to relax and accept the reality and complexity of these feelings in my soul.

I had been clutching my anxieties and had allowed the clamorous overload of information to seduce my soul into believing that there was a simple rational and physical solution to them. It was through the continued support of these friends nearby and many far away that I began to understand the importance of the third principle for restoring the soul.

Soul confirmation principle. As I acknowledge the complexity of my soul, I learn to overcome anxiety and accept love.

Soul confirmation is the act of acknowledging and accepting complex soul reactions and then confronting sensations that interfere with growth. As I began to understand the syncretistic nature of my soul and to accept the interdependence and holistic function of my being, I was able to confront the problems and confirm the process, the provision, and the potential of my soul.

SOUL PROBLEMS

Anxiety is a problem for my soul. It keeps me from focusing. It keeps me from loving. It spills over into the lives of those around me. It interferes with my communication with God. Bundling it inside is not the answer. It keeps spurting out at the most inconvenient times. Anxiety must be exposed as a problem.

Simply speaking aloud my anxious thoughts may be enough to confront and eliminate some minor anxieties. However, recurring thoughts that interfere with my daily activities require a more aggressive approach.

Writing down the specific cause of the anxiety is the first step in confronting it. I sometimes take a notepad and list each anxiety. It is amazing how the very action of writing out my concerns helps to clarify the issues I am dealing with.

In another column I may write a specific action that would help me with that anxiety. For instance, my struggle with separation anxiety was not based on reality. I am here and have *not* been separated from my family. I was projecting my feelings on my family and taking on what they might feel if I died. Since I believed that I would be with the Lord and unaffected by separation from those on earth, I was actually feeling a false sense of anxiety. The best thing that I can do for my family is to be present with them now and enjoy our time together, rather than mourning what could be.

This naming of my concerns before the Lord is the most important step in the confirmation of problems, especially of anxiety. Peter encouraged an even stronger action, while reminding us of God's care. He said: "Cast all your anxiety on him because he cares for you" (1 Peter 5:7).

First, I must acknowledge that the anxiety exists, that it is part of the complexity of my soul. Second, I need to be specific about what it is—even to writing it down. Third, I think of a specific action that would relieve the anxiety. And fourth, I bring the specifics of these problems to the Lord. I must give them to God. If the anxieties come back, I must give them to Him again.

Elizabeth Inrig, our pastor's wife and the Women's Ministry Director for both our church and the national conference of the Evangelical Free Church, shared her personal solution with us. She writes her anxieties on little pieces of paper and throws them in the trash can in her kitchen. What a great idea! The symbolic throwing away helps us to make the active choice of letting go of the problems.

I may choose to lay them on an altar or dispose of them in a waste can, but I need to discipline myself not to take those papers back. Can you imagine the foolishness of digging a paper out of the trash and saying, "I just want to worry about this one a little longer"?

If my anxieties return, and they do and they will, I may need to enlist the help of a friend or a counselor to understand exactly what is the cause and nature of my anxiety and how I can dispose of it.

Again:

1. I confirm the existence of my anxiety by naming it.
2. I confirm the cause of my anxiety by writing it down.
3. I confirm a solution by specifying a step I can take.
4. By prayer I present these anxieties to God.
5. As I release my anxieties by prayer, I physically release them by disposing of them.

SOUL PROCESS

In our first year of marriage, my husband and I attended the Seminar in Basic Youth Conflicts. One of the recurring themes that has stuck with me from that conference is: "God is not finished with me yet."

Sometimes, as we get older, it is easy to think that we are or should be completely spiritually mature—a finished product, you might say. One day as I was reading the book of Hebrews, I was struck in a new way with its message.

I was discouraged about my situation and the struggle my soul was having with accepting it. Then I read: "You have forgotten that word of encouragement that addresses you as sons" (Hebrews 12:5).

Encouragement?

The Scripture continues: "My son, do not make light of the Lord's discipline, and do not lose heart when he rebukes you, because the Lord disciplines those he loves, and he punishes everyone he accepts as a son" (Hebrews 12:5–6).

At first I remonstrated, "Why am I being punished? I've always tried to do the right thing."

I almost missed the blessing and lesson of the next verses: "Endure hardship as discipline; God is treating you as sons. For what son is not disciplined by his father?. . . No discipline seems pleasant at the time, but painful. Later on, however, it produces a harvest of righteousness and peace for those who have been trained by it" (Hebrews 12:7, 11).

When I began to see this time as a *training process* for my soul, I began to be excited. I didn't want to waste this time being anxious and complaining. Though I would not have chosen to have cancer, I did have it. I was already enrolled in this school. In my quiet moments alone, I realized how much I needed to grow spiritually. I could see sinful attitudes of selfishness, envy, even bitterness, lingering around, trying to take over.

Right there in the continuing verses of Hebrews were the words I needed to hear: "Therefore, strengthen the hands that are weak and the knees that are feeble, and make straight paths for your feet, so that the limb which is lame may not be put out of joint, but rather be healed" (Hebrews 12:12–13 NASB).

I needed to exercise the arms and knees of my soul.

"See to it," the passage continues, "that no one comes short of the grace of God; that no root of bitterness springing up causes trouble, and by it many be defiled" (Hebrews 12:15 NASB).

My soul began to awaken with delight when I realized that this experience was a wonderful process for the training of my inner person. I confirm the growth process by acknowledging that God's love for me as His child will allow me to grow through this human experience, rather than be squashed by it. I confirm the growth process by accepting His grace, as opposed to grumbling, as I walk through this human experience. God loves me so much that He will allow others to see a demonstration of His grace in my life. What an opportunity!

The exercise of confirming the process involves:

1. Giving thanks each day for the love and grace of God that allows me to be trained rather than trampled by this
2. Accepting other souls in process and allowing them to express their anxieties

There is so much I would miss if I did not confirm this as a process for my soul. I would miss the opportunity to know God's love and grace in a deeper way. I would miss the opportunity of confronting my own sinful attitudes, and thus I would be stifled in my growth. I would miss the opportunity of understanding and connecting with other souls in the process.

Through the exercise of soul confirmation I was learning to confirm God's provision for my soul.

SOUL PROVISION

As I gave my anxieties to God, I began to see His provision in many wonderful ways. I began to see how He was providing for the needs of my family. He continues to provide through His timing and the trust and gifts of friends.

Time was a big concern for me. When the process of treatment and surgery first began, our youngest daughter, Val, was a senior in high school. I prayed and asked others to pray that I would be able to attend her graduation. I prayed that I would not die before her graduation. I asked my doctor about how my treatments would fall around graduation time. By God's grace and the kind consideration of my doctor in planning treatments, I was there to rejoice with her at the Redlands Bowl as she marched triumphantly with her class.

Now, almost a year later, I look back at provision after provision of time with family. Our oldest daughter, Grace, was able to be at home for a number of weeks during the summer to plan her wedding. The timing of her wedding to our wonderful son-in-law, John Cosby, turned out to be some of my best weeks healthwise. Our son, Jon, decided to live at home and attend a local college this year, a timing that has been a blessing.

Trusted friends have relieved my imagination and maturation anxieties. For each family member, there is at least one other person praying for them regularly.

SOUL POTENTIAL

The exercise of soul confirmation allows me to soar beyond anxiety-imposed boundaries. As I release my problems, accepting the discipline of this process and God's provision of love and grace, I am able to express more love to others. As love pours out from our lives, the soul is strengthened with other qualities, for:

Love is patient, love is kind. It does not envy, it does not boast, it is not proud,

It is not rude, it is not self-seeking, it is not easily angered, it keeps no record of wrongs.

Love does not delight in evil but rejoices with the truth.

It always protects, always trusts, always hopes, always perseveres. (1 Corinthians 13:4–7)

CHOOSING TO MOVE BEYOND SURVIVAL

The book of Proverbs tells us that if we want wisdom we are to seek understanding and knowledge and our quest must equal the intensity of seeking silver and gold. It also tells me that, if I love my soul, I will seek wisdom.

> My son, if you accept my words
>   and store up my commands within you,
> turning your ear to wisdom and applying your heart
>   to understanding,
> and if you call out for insight
>   and cry aloud for understanding,
> and if you look for it as for silver
>   and search for it as for hidden treasure,
> then you will understand the fear of the Lord
>   and find the knowledge of God.
> For the Lord gives wisdom,
>   and from his mouth come knowledge and understanding.
>   (Proverbs 2:1–6)

Am I seeking through the discipline of this illness to understand how both the physical and emotional affect my soul? Am I seeking to know and understand the reality of pain and the growth process in other souls? Am I continuing to learn about the character of God and how He allows the human experience to become a divine experience in transforming the inner man?

SUMMARY

My goal in this exercise of soul confirmation is to acknowledge—and accept—the complex interactions of the soul and to confront the sensations that interfere with growth. I am motivated by the need to overcome anxiety and allow myself to accept and release love. Practical activities for reaching this goal include:

1. Writing down (naming) your anxieties
2. Confirming a solution by writing down a step you can take
3. Presenting your anxieties to God in prayer
4. Physically releasing your anxieties by disposing of the paper

The benefit of this exercise is that I am able to confront anxiety and move past it to experience the giving and receiving of love.

Chapter Four

SOUL INTERCESSION:
Confronting Impatience

J ust wait, and we'll call you," the receptionist instructed.

"You must change into a gown and wait here," the nurse explained.

"Wait for the doctor over there."

"Get dressed and wait for the test results."

"Wait on the line, and we'll schedule an appointment."

"We'll need to wait two or three months and then run that test again after you've had more treatments."

Just today, as I sat in the waiting room of the lab waiting for blood to be drawn, I listened to the frustration of other patients. A small elderly woman wearing a purple fleece jacket sat in a wheelchair. She sipped something from a paper cup and announced loudly, "I had a ten fifteen appointment this morning, but of course they didn't get to me until eleven thirty."

It was 12:45 P.M., and she was waiting again. "For a ride home," she said.

Another patient, a large man with a cast on his leg, was making explosive grumbling and sighing noises. His hair was disheveled, and his eyes were darting about nervously. When the clerk informed him that he would have to wait longer for a call from his doctor, he flailed his arms and muttered expletives. Then he proceeded to inform all of us that he had been there for an hour and a half.

I was sitting right across from him, and I paused in my reading, feeling apprehension. Was he going to hit someone? I wondered.

A few moments later, when a nurse called his name, he started to rise. But she quickly said, "No, no, don't get up. We have not been able to reach your doctor yet."

He flailed and swore again, while all others in the waiting room were silent and watching.

The nurse responded with great empathy and kindness in her tone, "I understand your frustration."

To everyone's relief, this disarmed him, and he listened to her explanation of the problem.

Waiting is difficult. Not only is it difficult on a daily basis, but in the long term it is especially trying. I could easily feel abandoned. I easily feel that my time has no value.

I am learning that waiting is the watchword of crisis. The life I knew waits in the wings, watching figures familiar to me mingle in unscripted scenes of drama and possible horror. Will this play never end?

THE WAITING RÉSUMÉ

It is not that I am unfamiliar with waiting. It is just that I thought I had done my share of waiting in life. I began to put together in my head a résumé of my waiting experience.

As a child, I was overly eager to pursue immediately the plans of life, and my mother taught me to repeat after her, "All things come to those who wait."

In college, my mind was already jumping ahead to my plans in the "real world." After graduation I joined Central American Mission International as a missionary and lived in Costa Rica and Mexico.

I waited until the age of thirty to marry Stuart. Then I waited to teach until our children were all of school age. I loved mothering, especially my three, and did not mind waiting to pursue other goals until they were grown.

52

More recently, I learned a new kind of waiting as a caregiver for older adults.

With all of that experience behind me, I thought I was good at waiting. After all, I knew from experience that "all things come to those who wait."

I knew how to keep my body still, waiting. Especially now, what else could I do? My body did not contain enough reserve energy to resist the waiting.

I thought that my mind and my emotions could be disciplined to wait in almost any circumstance. Just as I had learned to help my children long ago, I learned to prepare for the hours of waiting in offices and testing rooms by bringing a bag full of things to do.

Soon, however, I also learned that this crisis was much more than a waiting game to be outwitted by self-discipline. Unexpected negative patterns began to seep into my soul.

PATTERN OF IMPATIENCE

Time began to weave a thread through my days. My perception of wasted and lost time formed little knots and snags. I wanted to yank on the thread and make time pass faster. It was beyond me. I could not control time. Yielding to impatience made my soul slump. Ultimately I responded with either demands or discouragement.

We are influenced by our culture to demand our rights. I heard others in the waiting room loudly asking why they had not been called yet, announcing how many minutes they had been waiting or when they left home that morning, and I thought, *That could be me.*

I understood the feelings they were voicing. Time is a precious commodity to someone in my condition. When I think it may be taken away, I grasp harder to hold onto it. It represents the measure of my existence on this earth. I want it to count. Waiting seems to be a waste of time.

Beyond the daily wait, the big picture seemed to be stuck on Pause. It had been more than a year. Had I made any progress?

PATTERN OF ISOLATION

Alone and isolated, I turned my thoughts inward. *Why, when, and how will this end? What should I be doing? What will happen to me?* It is easy to become self-absorbed when in this condition. But introspection can strangle dreams and cause tension. The days of waiting, isolation, and solitude caused me to feel hemmed in. Friends would come to see me, but I was getting out less and less. Although the experience differs with each person and treatment, I found that, many days, I was physically limited by the side effects of treatment.

The waiting for appointments and treatments was coupled with the waiting to heal. Would this treatment make a difference? How long would it take?

Twice now we have experienced a major setback. After the initial three months of chemotherapy and surgery, we were looking to the next step, possibly a stem cell transplant and high dose chemotherapy at the City of Hope in Duarte, California. A few days after I had first seen the doctor at the City of Hope, I noticed a red rash at the site of the mastectomy. I saw my oncologist at Loma Linda that week, and he confirmed my fears. It was a surface recurrence of the cancer. In other words, those little red bumps were cancer lesions. A biopsy further confirmed this. We would have to wait for the City of Hope until this visible cancer was in full re-mission.

For six months I was on another chemotherapy treatment called Taxol. At first it seemed to help and was not quite as harsh on my system as earlier therapies. Then, for several weeks my blood counts were too low for me to receive therapy. During this time the lesions began to grow again. That meant we would have to try a different therapy to combat the cancer. As I write this, fortunately, it appears that the latest treatment is beginning to help. It is now more than fifteen months since my cancer was first discovered.

During this long wait, it has been a continuing struggle for me to adjust to isolation and limitations. It has always been a joy for me to be involved with people. I would go to them. Now I have to wait for friends to come to me. Often visits are limited because my blood counts are low, and friends are concerned about exposing me to germs.

Though some solitude can be a blessing, when it is the pattern of life —day after day after day—it can be boring and unbearable. I struggle with the desire to do worthwhile things, to continue meaningful relationships.

PATTERN OF CRITICISM

Separated in that world of self, I fell into a pattern of critical thinking. There is so much *time* to think. Without my realizing what was happening, the intense analysis of self suddenly turned into a negative analysis of others. I began to feel disconnected from others. Feeling that my experience was unique and my opportunities so limited, my soul searched for perfection in myself and others and ended up perforating the patterns of good relationships.

SOUL INTERCESSION

What was happening? My soul was cooped up inside myself and acting out as though it had a bad case of cabin fever. Maybe that was the problem—confinement to myself. Struggling to find a way to exercise my soul during this waiting period, I began to learn the secret of soul waiting. And by learning this secret, I started to experience the fourth principle for restoring the soul.

The fourth principle. As I extend my soul through intercession for others, I am able to move beyond impatience and experience joy.

I began to learn that the exercise of soul intercession is the action of involvement in and intervention for the personal needs of others. I began to learn the joy of really listening to others. Since I was so isolated, I did not have a great deal to talk about concerning my own activities. So I just sat back and listened.

Intentional listening, without the need to respond, allowed me to hear more than just the words others were saying. I heard the meaning. I noticed what was not said. I heard joy, and I heard pain. Yes, because of the pain I was experiencing, in a new way I was able to hear others' pain.

Many times friends would begin to tell me about a sorrow or difficulty in their lives and then quickly interject, "I know this is nothing compared to your pain."

I didn't feel that way. My pain helped me to realize that pain is pain. Though the body may experience different levels of pain, the one experiencing emotional pain hurts just the same. Coming to that understanding helped me to empathize with others. Listening became an exercise of extending my soul.

Hospitality is an action of involvement that I have always enjoyed. I could not entertain now. It was just too much. Aunt Jean came all the way from Richmond, Virginia, and helped me as a caregiver for many weeks. Her actions of hospitality in answering my phone, welcoming visitors, and explaining when I was too weak to receive them, have been a great blessing. As a caregiver, she intervened and released me to enjoy what I could, while not having to carry the responsibility for receiving visitors. As she exercised her gift of hospitality, both of us were able to extend our souls to others. Personal intervention and involvement is an experience and exercise of soul intercession. This is also an opportunity for the caregiver. My dear Stuart has been the most helpful in this area.

Stuart is my advocate. In my weakened condition, there are many tasks that I feel unable to handle. He goes before me in a wonderful way, taking care of what I cannot. I am so blessed by his presence and love. His personal intervention and involvement is an experience and exercise in soul intercession.

For me, prayer has become the greatest experience in soul intercession. As I listen to needs, I begin to pray for friends in more specific ways. For instance, before my illness I did not realize that my friend Carol continually battled pain in her knees. When she first came to visit me, she shared two verses that I wanted to remember so I wrote them on three-by-five cards. They were:

> May our Lord Jesus Christ himself and God our Father, who loved us and by his grace gave us eternal encouragement and good hope,
> encourage your hearts and strengthen you in every good deed and word. (2 Thessalonians 2:16–17)

> I pray also that the eyes of your heart may be enlightened in order that you may know the hope to which he has called you, the riches of his glorious inheritance in the saints,
> and his incomparably great power for us who believe. That power is like the working of his mighty strength,
> which he exerted in Christ when he raised him from the dead and seated him at his right hand in the heavenly realms,

far above all rule and authority, power and dominion, and every title that can be given, not only in the present age but also in the one to come. (Ephesians 1:18–21)

On the back of the verse cards I wrote her name. Then, when I carried the cards with me to appointments, I would not only review the Scriptures but pray for her. As others shared specific verses with me, I wrote them down with the name of my friend on the back of the card. Soon I was asking these friends how I could pray more specifically for them and writing that down. The more I prayed, the more interested I was in keeping in touch to see how they were doing.

I have asked family members and others to share verses with me. Both the Scriptures and their requests have given me encouragement and joy in interceding for them. Prayer is one of the greatest experiences in soul intercession.

As an exercise of intercession for others, three activities led me down the path to patience and satisfaction.

The activity of attentive listening. By carefully listening to others, I learn of their personal needs, I am drawn closer to them, and I am able to intercede more specifically for them.

The activity of hospitality. Welcoming people to my home, no matter what the condition, allows me the opportunity to listen and enjoy the details of their lives. It also helps them to understand my condition and to intercede for me. There is satisfaction in mutual intercession, one for another.

The activity of prayer. My commitment to pray for others allows me to be actively involved in their lives, even though I have limited physical energy. As I watch and learn how God is answering my prayers, I learn to trust Him, and He gives me patience. I know that He hears me and that His timing is perfect. I can fill the hours of waiting with prayers of petition and praise.

Using the Scriptures as a guide for prayer and praise has taught me patience and brought me great joy. Many of the Psalms have been a basis for my prayers. A few of them follow:

Turn my heart toward your statutes
    and not toward selfish gain.
Turn away my eyes from worthless things;
    preserve my life according to your word.
Fulfill your promise to your servant,
    so that you may be feared.
Take away the disgrace I dread,
    for your laws are good.
How I long for your precepts!
    Preserve my life in your righteousness.
(Psalm 119:36–40)

Your hands made me and formed me;
    Give me understanding to learn your commands.
May those who fear you rejoice when they see me,
    for I have put my hope in your word.
I know, O Lord, that your laws are righteous,
    and in faithfulness you have afflicted me.
May your unfailing love be my comfort,
    according to your promise to your servant.
Let your compassion come to me that I may live,
    for your law is my delight.
(Psalm 119:73–77)

I have hidden your word in my heart
    that I might not sin against you.
Praise be to you, O Lord;
    teach me your decrees.
(Psalm 119:11–12)

These Scriptures are an encouragement to my soul. What I am learning, though, is that soul intercession goes beyond soul encouragement. While intercession is the *action of intervening*, in a deeper sense it is entreating in favor of another. This is the activity that revives my soul—when I am willing to put myself on the line for another and speak on his behalf.

I had to ask myself, do I routinely go through a list of requests for others, or do I really intercede for them before others and the Lord? The Scriptures give us five interesting pictures of intercession.

PICTURE ONE: BUSINESS INTERCESSION

In Genesis 23 we learn that Abraham's wife Sarah died in the land of Canaan. Abraham was heartbroken, and as he wept for her, he realized that he needed to purchase a burial site. So he spoke to the Hittites who lived there: "I am an alien and a stranger among you. Sell me some property for a burial site here so I can bury my dead" (v. 4).

The Hittites replied that he was a mighty prince among them and none of them would refuse him. So what did Abraham do? He said, "If you are willing to let me bury my dead, then listen to me and intercede with Ephron son of Zohar on my behalf so he will sell me the cave of Machpelah, which belongs to him and is at the end of his field" (vv. 8–9).

The next verse reveals what was said in the negotiations between Abraham and Zohar, so we must assume that the Hittites prepared the way. The point is that someone had to be willing to speak on his behalf, to vouch for his integrity, to intercede.

Am I willing to intercede for another in a business deal, in a matter other than physical and spiritual needs? Am I involved enough in another's life? Do I care enough?

PICTURE TWO: BEYOND INTERCESSION

A second picture in the Old Testament is that of the priest Eli and his sons. Eli was troubled because of the reported wicked deeds of his sons. He spoke to them:

> No, my sons; it is not a good report that I hear spreading among the Lord's people.
> If a man sins against another man, God may mediate for him; but if a man sins against the Lord, who will intercede for him? (1 Samuel 2:24–25)

His sons did not repent. "His sons, however, did not listen to their father's rebuke" (v. 25).

Does this mean that Eli did not intercede for them? We do not know. Since he was a parent, it seems almost sure that he did entreat the Lord for them. Does that mean that we should not intercede for some people? In the sense of vouching for their integrity, we cannot. Should we intercede for their salvation? Yes.

It is easy, though, to think that some are beyond intercession. As I have been convicted about the meaning (and work) of intercession, I believe that only God knows who is resisting and "beyond intercession." For me to "give up" on someone is an act of laziness and disbelief.

PICTURE THREE: CONDITIONAL INTERCESSION

Samuel asked the Israelites to rid themselves of foreign gods and the Ashtaroth. These were the Canaanite fertility goddess and the female counterparts of Baal. Canaanite cultic religion had become part of Israelite worship. And this was the condition that Samuel laid down before he would intercede for them. 1 Samuel 7:4–5 states that "the Israelites put away their Baals and Ashtaroths, and served the Lord only. Then Samuel said, 'Assemble all Israel at Mizpah and I will intercede with the Lord for you.'"

When I make a commitment to intercede for another soul, I must be close enough to and care enough about him or her to speak about obvious sin. I am learning that intercession is serious spiritual business. I must be willing to put my reputation on the line for the one for whom I am interceding.

PICTURE FOUR: PERFECT INTERCESSION

One day when I was fretting about who would intercede for my family if I were not here, my friend Elizabeth reminded me of a wonderful truth that has been such a comfort to my soul. *Jesus* is continually interceding for us before the Father.

> But because Jesus lives forever, he has a permanent priesthood.
> Therefore he is able to save completely those who come to God through him, because he always lives to intercede for them. (Hebrews 7:24–25)

60

Romans 8:31–34 reveals this same truth:

> If God is for us, who can be against us?
> He who did not spare his own Son, but gave him up for us all—how will he not also, along with him, graciously give us all things?
> Who will bring any charge against those whom God has chosen? It is God who justifies.
> Who is he that condemns? Christ Jesus, who died—more than that, who was raised to life—is at the right hand of God and is also interceding for us.

And the Spirit intercedes for us:

> In the same way, the Spirit helps us in our weakness. We do not know what we ought to pray for, but the Spirit himself intercedes for us with groans that words cannot express.
> And he who searches our hearts knows the mind of the Spirit, because the Spirit intercedes for the saints in accordance with God's will. (Romans 8:26–27)

From these biblical pictures I am learning that soul intercession is not an activity to be entered into lightly but with commitment and compassion. When I choose to truly intercede for another, I am blessed with patience and satisfaction.

CHOOSING TO MOVE BEYOND SURVIVAL

Mutual intercession, each one helping and praying for the other, is an experience that moves us beyond survival and offers us the blessing of learning patience and experiencing satisfaction.

It is interesting to note in the New Testament book of James three characteristics of patience:

1. Not grumbling against each other (5:7–9)
2. Persevering (5:10–11)
3. Not swearing (5:12)

How true it is that often, when we observe signs of impatience, we hear grumbling and swearing and see the tendency to give up.

Is James proposing the antidote to impatience in James 5:13–18? Are these all actions of intercession?

> Is any one of you in trouble? He should pray. Is anyone happy? Let him sing songs of praise.
>
> Is any one of you sick? He should call the elders of the church to pray over him and anoint him with oil in the name of the Lord.
>
> And the prayer offered in faith will make the sick person well; the Lord will raise him up. If he has sinned, he will be forgiven.
>
> Therefore, confess your sins to each another and pray for each other so that you may be healed. The prayer of a righteous man is powerful and effective.
>
> Elijah was a man just like us. He prayed earnestly that it would not rain, and it did not rain on the land for three and a half years.
>
> Again he prayed, and the heavens gave rain, and the earth produced its crops.

SUMMARY

My goal in this exercise is to become involved with and intervene for the personal needs of others. My desire is to overcome impatience by loving others effectively. Practical activities for reaching this goal include: listening attentively, extending hospitality, and praying—specifically using the idea of prayer cards. The benefit of this exercise is that I am able to overcome impatience and experience joy.

Chapter Five

SOUL RESTORATION:
Confronting Pride, Envy, and Denial

Dreams are like the mountains rising majestically before me, offering to lift me above the valley of despair to the pure heights of all possibilities. My dreams pull together all the pieces of my being, offering a sense of completion and significance to my existence.

Looking at the beautiful mountains surrounding our home, I think about my dreams of the past and wonder about future dreams. Are my dreams my soul's tomorrows? I have asked myself this question in an effort to sort out the meaning of fulfillment today. Other questions to be considered come to mind. Can I dream again? How do I begin? Does "restoration" mean the revival of dreams?

ARE MY DREAMS MY SOUL'S TOMORROWS?

I think my dreams are my tomorrows. Yet, my tomorrows are uncertain. Is it possible to live with satisfaction today without reference to or thought of tomorrow's dreams?

On the one hand, I agree with the psalmist: "This is the day the Lord has made; let us rejoice and be glad in it" (Psalm 118:24).

On the other hand, my mind is always anticipating the future: "Therefore prepare your minds for action" (1 Peter 1:13).

I must live on a dual track, rejoicing and making the most of today, yet always preparing for tomorrow. Is that preparation a part of dream making?

I have realized during this time of crisis how much of my today is predicated on my vision of tomorrow. Dreaming is building, working toward goals, reaching pinnacles of satisfaction. Yet sometimes I struggle with both a lack of feeling joy and a lack of being able to dream. How can I dream about tomorrow when today may be all that I have?

I think about the dreams that Stuart and I have talked about.

One involves a practice we started years ago—that of encouraging our friends in Costa Rica and Guatemala to send their children to us for extended visits to provide opportunity for learning English.

Would we ever be able to do that again? I wondered.

I think of five wonderful young boys, Angel Rodrigo, Daniel Alejandro, Pablo Guillermo, Daniel Estuardo, and Jose Carlos, whose grandparents Angelica and Daniel Figueroa were colleagues of Stuart's in Guatemala in years past. I dream of their coming to stay with us on their vacations just as the previous generation—Chiqui, Carlos, and Beth—had.

I dream another dream of my own children, one just married and two single, attending college. I anticipate watching them develop independent lives and ministries, visiting their homes, perhaps baby-sitting their children someday.

These and other dreams are intertwined with my loving husband, who envisions with me how we will together give our time and shared experiences to helping others in the future. Maybe we will have a retreat center. We can imagine a Spanish Mediterranean-style refuge, where families or individuals would come to be refreshed and renewed. Maybe we will continue service in education also. Maybe we will minister in a Spanish-speaking church. Maybe we will return to Central America.

Are my dreams my soul's tomorrows? If so, perhaps I need to refocus my question to ask, "Can I dream again?"

CAN I DREAM AGAIN?

As weeks of treatment turned into months, my dreams became distorted like bursting bubbles. When my cancer continued to grow, I felt my dreams were dying.

Can I learn to dream again? I continued to wonder.

There is no feeling, no inspiration, no thought space for dreams when I am experiencing soul pain.

Without my realizing it, anger was keeping me from dreaming. Anger was difficult for me to recognize because I did not shout or deny God. More subtly, anger took on the form of three perceived dream busters that barred me from creating new dreams by keeping me isolated, clouding my perspective, and obscuring reality. They were pride, envy, and denial.

PRIDE CAUSES ISOLATION

It was so difficult for me to recognize that I struggled with pride that it took me many, many months to name it. I told people that I was struggling with being too tough. In a sense, I guess I was proud of my pride.

I can tough this out, I thought.

Pride begins with little things. There was one area that I was especially proud about: controlling pain. I had watched some others going through pain. They moaned and groaned continually and could never be comforted.

"I will not do that to my family," I decided.

So I gritted my teeth and refused to take sufficient pain medication after surgery. It was difficult to admit I needed help. I was proud and perhaps in a way angry to be in a situation that I could not control.

My dear Aunt Jean was staying with me, helping me in every way. She talked to me about not waiting until the pain was unbearable. She and my friend Carol patiently talked me through my muddle with medication. I finally listened.

Carol suggested a little chart, using numbers one to five. I monitored my pain throughout the day, using one as "no pain" and five as "excruciating pain." The numbers in between were labeled "some," "bearable," "uncomfortable." I had been waiting until level five to take medication and was not getting enough relief to sleep. One would think that, as an adult, I could have figured out that would not work.

Through this incident I began to think about the positives and negatives of control and how it can grow out of hand. It can invade our lives, keeping us from trusting others and God. On the positive side, self-control is a scriptural command. There is dignity in control, and—particularly in a physical crisis—the soul needs to have some degree of control. Taking all control away from my soul in crisis strips me of the incentive to carry on. Therefore, the dignity of self-control is good. It allows me to be who I am and to pursue what I want to be.

I was troubled, though, by a subtle inner warning: While keeping the door open for dignity, I needed to watch out that pride did not push its way through. Pride huffs and puffs and bursts dreams. It isolates me from the spiritual relationships that encourage my dreams. Pride destroys my ability to dream by bringing in a high wind, lifting me up in the moment of control only to let me down to feel loneliness and despair as it moves on to blow through yet another soul.

How could I confront pride and restore trust in my soul?

ENVY CLOUDS PERSPECTIVE

"You can be angry. It's all right," my friend said.

"But I'm not. I'm not angry," I responded.

I did not recognize it, but anger was taking on the guise of envy and striking my soul like lightning at the most unexpected moments. It took the form of comparison.

I wouldn't wish this on anyone else, but why did I get cancer and he or she didn't? I'd silently question. I'd never smoked or drank. I had my mammograms. I took care of all the sick people. I didn't deserve this.

At the oddest moments, thoughts about people I didn't even know personally, but knew about through the media, would flash through my mind.

Look how that person has abused his body. And he doesn't have cancer. Look how that woman displays herself, taking her healthy body for granted, I would think.

Of course no one deserves cancer. It is not a punishment. But envy and anger had slipped in the back door of my soul. And envy is an evil dream buster that twists the soul, confusing my perception of life, keeping me from trusting God.

DENIAL DISGUISES REALITY

A third dream buster was even more confusing, because it wrapped itself in the robe of positive thinking. It came in the guise of denial.

"If I function as a well person, I will be a well person," I convinced myself.

But denial can result in overlooking obvious needs—for practical help, for emotional and spiritual support, for soul restoration.

Short-term denial seems to work. That is why we use it to soothe our souls. But as the days go on and on and on, and my problem seems to worsen instead of get better, denial pierces my soul. It not only brushes aside reality in relationship to my central problem, but it slowly destroys my relationship to other areas of reality.

It was in the practical everyday things that I had trouble accepting reality at first.

My friend and neighbor Donna offered to help organize meals for our family. During the early months of my treatment that first winter and spring, I was most grateful for this help. The women of our church were overwhelmingly generous, too. (There are some great cooks among them.) Though I continued chemotherapy in the summer (then fall, winter, and spring again), I came to a point where I began to feel guilty about accepting all this generosity. "They will not understand. They will think less of you," denial told me.

"I should be more responsible and independent. I can cook," I told Stuart.

Donna was not convinced. "Are you sure?" she asked.

"Oh, yes, we're fine."

If I functioned as a well person, I would be a well person, I had convinced myself. Denial was prancing around in a borrowed robe.

Sometimes the deeper we go into denial, the more we cut off others and lead a solitary existence. Donna saw the masquerade and wisely pointed out to me my need for some help.

Little by little I learned to accept help, but finally recognizing how my condition would affect our future was the most difficult process for me.

For a long time, I could not handle the possibility that I would die unless the doctors could stop this cancer—or God sent a miracle of healing. Our surgeon wisely urged us to recognize the facts—that statistics did not favor life—and to allow ourselves to grieve. Our souls battled against his words, but our emotions caved in. The grieving was a release and, though difficult, emotionally cleansing.

Instead of helping us to get on with our lives, denial had burst our dreams by ignoring the pain of our souls. The desire to have a positive focus sometimes caused us to deny the agony within, the pain of thinking about permanent earthly separation, death. Once we were able to face that which we thought would be the worst outcome of this struggle, and talk about that, we were able to release some of the tension that the denial of secret fear creates.

I always thought that it was the fact that I might die that kept me from dreaming today, but I discovered that it was not an anticipated physical barrier that kept me from dreams. It was a spiritual barrier. When I am in denial, I find it impossible to accept the spiritual and emotional support of friends and family around me. My spirit retreats, and denial stands between me and my dreams.

Our children have helped me break the barrier of denial with their encouraging statements:

"We want to know the truth."

"Do not keep things from us in an effort to protect us."

"God is providing for our needs."

What reassurance and comfort and release it is to hear those words!

As long as I live in denial, it is impossible for me to experience soul restoration because denial refuses to recognize weakness.

Pride, envy, and denial have created confusion in my soul. Before I can find restoration, I must undergo a confrontation and accept resolution. I am still learning this, so as I share this process, you will be given a glimpse of a very private moving in my soul. This is not easy to reveal to you or to myself. However, God willing, we will see a moving of His Spirit together.

HOW DO I BEGIN?

The process that I am going to describe is based on the principle of soul restoration.

The fifth principle. As I release my soul to God and enter into His presence, I am able to trust and experience faithfulness and gentleness.

Soul restoration involves "entering the sanctuary"—an activity that stretches the soul beyond ritual worship to embrace the very presence of God. I could not let go of this concept of entering the sanctuary after reading Psalm 73 one day. It jumped out from the pages of my Bible, speaking words that I had dared to think. The early part of the psalm aptly describes feelings that I had had in my state of confusion.

> But as for me, my feet had almost slipped;
> > I had nearly lost my foothold.
> For I envied the arrogant
> > when I saw the prosperity of the wicked.
> They have no struggles;
> > their bodies are healthy and strong.
> They are free from the burdens common to man;
> > they are not plagued by human ills. . . .
> Surely in vain have I kept my heart pure;
> > in vain have I washed my hands in innocence.
> All day long I have been plagued;
> > I have been punished every morning. . . .
> When I tried to understand all this,
> > it was oppressive to me
> till I entered the sanctuary of God;
> > then I understood their final destiny.
> > > (Psalm 73:2–5,13–14,16–17)

I was so moved by the entire chapter that I read it several times. As I did, I began to see the relationship between restoration, "entering the sanctuary," and the revival of dreams. The pivotal point seemed to be "entering the sanctuary," and I thought for many days about what that means.

What happens in the "sanctuary" that pulls me out of my confusion? What *is* the sanctuary, and what does it mean to enter the sanctuary? Is the sanctuary a physical building, a spiritual refuge, or a safe place for my soul? God's inspired Word gives insight into these questions. From His Word I am learning three truths: Confrontation opens the door, resolution occurs within the sanctuary, and restoration is the result of trust.

CONFRONTATION OPENS THE DOOR

It is difficult when experiencing an extremely undesirable, seemingly undeserved, megacrisis in life to assess oneself honestly and repent of sin. I came to such a low point in my physical crisis that it seemed impossible to face the reality that other areas of my life were not perfect. It was just too much to handle.

When I compare myself to others and continue to deny anger, envy, and pride—whether silently or allowing words to slip from my tongue—I ignore the infection of sin in my soul. Although this cancer is not a punishment for my sin, my soul will not be cleansed without confrontation and confession of sin. I cannot enter "the sanctuary," the place of restoration, with unclean hands.

Psalm 15 speaks to this directly:

> Lord, who may dwell in your sanctuary?
>   Who may live on your holy hill?
> He whose walk is blameless
>   and who does what is righteous,
> who speaks the truth from his heart
>   and has no slander on his tongue,
> who does his neighbor no wrong
>   and casts no slur on his fellowman,
> who despises a vile man
>   but honors those who fear the Lord,
> who keeps his oath
>   even when it hurts,
> who lends his money without usury
>   and does not accept a bribe
>   against the innocent.
> He who does these things
>   will never be shaken.

The power of these words, particularly in my current situation, is immense. "He who does these things will never be shaken." At the same time that I confront the sin that will keep me from "entering the sanctuary," I am given the promise of restoration. *"He who does these things will never be shaken."* Never shaken? What a gem this is, glistening in the sanctuary.

It is also clear that, with unconfessed known sin, I cannot benefit from the promise of the sanctuary, for I cannot dwell there. Psalm 24 announces similar conditions for entering this holy place.

> Who may ascend the hill of the Lord?
> Who may stand in his holy place?
> He who has clean hands and a pure heart,
> who does not lift up his soul to an idol
> or swear by what is false.
> He will receive blessing from the Lord
> and vindication from God his Savior.
> (Psalm 24:3–5)

"Good" people have a hard time confronting sins such as pride, envy, and denial. It is not as if I were an ax murderer (uh-oh—comparison and pride sweep through my soul again). What often happens in my life is that I end up apologizing to God for my weaknesses instead of confronting sin.

Confrontation of sin must go beyond an apology. This is what I am learning again. I must confess and repent. My initial confession and repentance of sin as a child, and my acceptance of the sacrificial death and resurrection of Jesus Christ for my salvation, sealed my relationship to God as His child. My crisis reveals my immaturity. I question what God is doing. I complain and compare myself to the "really" wicked. My soul spins in a circle of confusion, far from quiet, far from rest. It is lonely, isolated, and afraid.

I tend to look at Christian giants and think, *They have no sin. I want to be like him or her, mature, pouring out spiritual advice, a blessing to others.*

I know that my mentors and models also struggle with sin, but it is so easy to see them as truly sanctified. I think I must reach that point in this life, and it is tempting to merely apologize or deny sin. The first letter of John in the New Testament puts this clearly in perspective. He is speaking to the believer in Christ:

> If we claim to be without sin, we deceive ourselves and the truth is not in us.
> If we confess our sins, he is faithful and just and will forgive us our sins and purify us from all unrighteousness.
> If we claim we have not sinned, we make him out to be a liar and his word has no place in our lives.

> My dear children, I write this to you so that you will not sin.
> But if anybody does sin, we have one who speaks to the Father in
> our defense—Jesus Christ, the Righteous One.
>
> He is the atoning sacrifice for our sins, and not only for ours
> but also for the sins of the whole world. (1 John 1:8–10; 2:1–2)

Though God in His grace knows my struggle, I cannot ignore or merely apologize for sin. True confrontation of sin involves confession and repentance.

The Weight of Your Words, by Joseph Stowell, is a book that has meaningfully instructed me again and again. The title alone tells me what I must do if I truly repent: keep my tongue in check. For me that means just saying no to the unspoken words that rumble through my soul. I must learn to interrupt those unrighteous thoughts and replace them with the positive and the good.

It is through divine strength, then, that I enter into the sanctuary, for God is the One who cleanses and strengthens me to turn from sin to doing good. Therefore, when I wish to enter the sanctuary, a safe place, a refuge where I am alone in His presence, I must confront my sin.

Then, as I enter through the doors, I am filled with praise and thanksgiving for who He is and what He does. I feel that a simple thank You is not enough; I must find new ways to worship and adore Him. Scriptures, hymns, praise songs, listening, stillness, rest, restoration—all of these are part of my soul experience in the sanctuary, that is, in His presence.

Psalm 68 gives us a glimpse into the sanctuary:

> Your procession has come into view, O God,
>> the procession of my God and King into the sanctuary.
> In front are the singers, after them the musicians;
>> with them are the maidens playing tambourines.
> Praise God in the great congregation.
>
> (Psalm 68:24–26)

Does this view of God take place in the physical edifice called the sanctuary, the church? Sometimes yes, and sometimes no. Sometimes I struggle with distractions in the building called the sanctuary. Usually that means that I have not seriously prepared to "enter the sanctuary" and have merely gone into a building. If we want to truly "enter the sanctuary" at any time or place, we must recognize the gravity of stepping through the doorway. We cannot enter with unclean hands.

ENTRANCE CREATES RESOLUTION

I am still in process, but as I seek God's direction in "entering the sanctuary," I believe four changes take place. They are:

1. A change of person
2. A change of place or presence
3. A change of perception
4. A change of power

Change of person. My person is changed as my soul releases not only the weight of its sin but also the unnecessary burdens that it carries around.

My dreams, for instance, can become a dead weight. If I am constantly lamenting the loss of the unchangeable, it is as if I am carrying the ashes of my dead dreams about with me. I cannot carry them into the sanctuary. Why do I hold onto them? I beg God to bring them back to life. In doing so, my soul is acting out conflicting desires. No wonder I am so confused.

It is as if I am saying, "I know You are all-powerful, God, to work out everything my way."

Yes, I know that I must release the ashes of my former dreams and trust Him, but I cautiously guard the ashes, asking myself if I can give these up.

Can I trust Him with my ashes?

Until I am willing to release the ashes of my past dreams, I am stuck at the entrance of the sanctuary, unable to move into the inner court. As I let go of the ashes, I trust God to create new dreams in my soul.

I cannot even comprehend the measure of trust Abraham demonstrated in releasing his dreams for his son Isaac. He had waited for years to have a child, a boy. When God asked him to sacrifice his only son, all of his dreams died. They were turned to ashes. But as he stood before God, he did not beg Him to give back his dreams. Instead, he said in essence, "I trust you, God, to create new dreams." Instead of begging God not to take his dream, he released it. He did so by intentionally moving forward in trust.

And as Abraham demonstrated his trust by releasing his dreams, he was changed.

Change of place or presence. Where is the sanctuary my soul seeks? Is it merely a safe place, a refuge?

We often call our place of worship the sanctuary. In Old Testament times there was a literal sanctuary built by God's people as a place of sacrifice and worship. It was a sacred place where only those ordained by God were allowed to enter the inner rooms. These were the priests, the mediators between God and man. Though man could enter the sanctuary, he could not cross the veil into the Holy of Holies.

God's people entered the sanctuary because there they met the presence of God. God's presence in the sanctuary is declared in the Psalms:

> May the Lord answer you when you are in distress;
> > may the name of the God of Jacob protect you.
> May he send you help from the sanctuary
> > and grant you support from Zion.
> > > (Psalm 20:1–2)

> You are awesome, O God, in your sanctuary.
> > > (Psalm 68:35)

Today, through Jesus, we may enter God's presence without a priest or a physical building:

> We who have fled to take hold of the hope offered
> > to us may be greatly encouraged.
> We have this hope as an anchor for the soul, firm and secure.
> > It enters the inner sanctuary behind the curtain,
> where Jesus, who went before us, has entered on our behalf.
> > He has become a high priest forever, in the order of Melchizedek.
> > > (Hebrews 6:18–20)

When we "enter the sanctuary" through prayer and worship, we enter the very presence of God. His presence is a safe place, a refuge, a good place.

> But as for me, it is good to be near God.
> I have made the sovereign Lord my refuge;
> I will tell of all your deeds.
>
> (Psalm 73:28)

The psalmist was referring to his experience in the sanctuary. I learn that it is good. I learn that the writer has released his ashes. His "heart was grieved" and his "spirit embittered," yet he turned from his dreams to trust God. I learn once again that I can trust because God is sovereign. I learn that the evidence of this trust is praise, the telling of God's deeds.

Change of perception. In God's presence I finally understand the big picture. Before I entered the sanctuary, I was narrowly focused on myself and my problems, seeing others only in comparison to myself.

But what happens in the sanctuary involves far more than merely disciplining myself to see the greater picture in life. My perception is not changed because I see more of the world. It is changed because I see Him, the sovereign Lord. I see the perfection of His character, His righteousness, His justice, His loving-kindness, His faithfulness. I trust Him.

David beautifully described his experience of entering the sanctuary:

> O God, you are my God,
> earnestly I seek you;
> my soul thirsts for you,
> my body longs for you,
> in a dry and weary land
> where there is no water.
> I have seen you in the sanctuary
> and beheld your power and your glory.
> Because your love is better than life,
> my lips will glorify you.

75

I will praise you as long as I live,
and in your name I will lift up my hands.
My soul will be satisfied
as with the richest of foods;
with singing lips my mouth will praise you.
On my bed I remember you;
I think of you through the watches
of the night.
Because you are my help,
I sing in the shadow of your wings.
My soul clings to you;
your right hand upholds me.

(Psalm 63:1–8)

Change of power. I am a changed person, changed by God's presence, with a changed perception. And, wonderfully, in the sanctuary I am changed by God's power.

In Psalm 73, again we see who is in control of my soul through this experience. The psalmist speaks to God.

Yet I am always with you;
you hold me by my right hand.
You guide me with your counsel,
and afterward you will take me into glory.
Whom have I in heaven but you?
And earth has nothing I desire besides you.
My flesh and my heart may fail,
but God is the strength of my heart
and my portion forever.

(Psalm 73:23–26)

He holds my hand. He guides and counsels me. He is the strength of my soul.

WHAT DOES RESTORATION MEAN?

What actually happens in my life when I come to the point of trusting the sovereign God? The soul that was formerly overwhelmed, feeling almost dead, is restored.

My heavy soul emerges rested.

My sorrowful soul emerges rejoicing.

My defeated soul emerges triumphant.

My confused soul emerges calm.

When I release the burden of my ashes, my soul is restored. Jesus says, "Come to me, all you who are weary and burdened, and I will give you rest. Take my yoke upon you and learn from me, for I am gentle and humble in heart, and you will find rest for your souls. For my yoke is easy and my burden is light" (Matthew 11:28–30).

As I release to God my sorrow, I expectantly await joy: "Restore to me the joy of your salvation and grant me a willing spirit" (Psalm 51:12).

Though I feel bitter and defeated, God will triumphantly restore my hope: "Though you have made me see troubles, many and bitter, you will restore my life again; from the depths of the earth you will again bring me up" (Psalm 71:20).

When I feel confused and overloaded, God leads me to quietness. "He makes me lie down in green pastures, he leads me beside quiet waters, he restores my soul" (Psalm 23:2–3).

The exercise of soul restoration that results from "entering the sanctuary" encourages my soul to pursue three specific disciplines.

First, I desire to gain more knowledge and understanding of the sovereignty of God. I see His sovereignty from a new perspective when I "enter the sanctuary." With increased knowledge, I do not view Him as a tyrannical God, imposing a difficult structure or circumstance upon me. Instead I see Him as a loving and awesomely powerful God whom I can trust.

Second, I desire to praise God in every way possible. I seek new ways and opportunities to praise Him. I realize that all my dreams must revolve around praising Him.

Third, I learn to view other souls with compassion, not comparison. When I am tempted to be envious or critical, I confront and repent of my sin. I seek to understand more fully the complexities and needs of other souls—and to understand their pain. By God's grace this helps me to reach out with gentleness.

These three disciplines teach me more of God and lead me to trust His faithfulness. As I trust Him, my soul is released from my burdens and infused with new creative energy. Quietly, new dreams begin to form. They are dreams unrestricted by events, time, belongings, and people. They are spiritually nurtured dreams—reviving the soul.

CHOOSING TO MOVE BEYOND SURVIVAL

The dream busters pride, envy, and denial whisper yet another falsehood in my ears. They tell me that my soul does not matter. They urge me to be tough. "Don't trust God," they say. "Just take *whatever*."

"But my soul is thirsty, and dry, and dying," I plead.

The dream busters do not care. They reply, "After all, we are tolerant, so—*whatever*."

My soul gasps. "*Whatever*—what does that mean?"

Do I dare exchange my soul for just whatever?

Jesus said, "What good will it be for a man if he gains the whole world, yet forfeits his soul? Or what can a man give in exchange for his soul?" (Matthew 16:26).

My soul does matter. When I "enter the sanctuary," in God's presence I see the value of my soul. I see His righteousness and will stand for absolutes and righteousness. I see His love and will allow Him to love through me. I see His faithfulness, and my faith is revived.

SUMMARY

My goal is to confront pride, envy, and anger, and release my soul to God. My desire is that He will restore my soul. Practical activities for reaching this goal include: pursuing knowledge of God, praising His sovereignty, and thinking with compassion, not comparison. The benefit of this exercise is that I will learn to trust and experience His faithfulness and gentleness.

Chapter Six

SOUL CONNECTION:
Confronting Hopelessness

*I*t's hopeless!"

These are words anyone dreads to hear. There are moments when my soul sinks into despair and I wonder, *Is there hope?*

As friends and even strangers offer words of comfort and hope, I notice words that are familiar, because I too have used them. But now I scrutinize them in a new light.

"You have the hope of eternal life," is one statement.

"Don't lose your hope," another reminds me.

"If you have hope, you have life," concludes a third.

I am at a loss to respond to these benign comments, while fully recognizing their good intent. I listen skeptically because I am not sure how it changes the prognosis for my life. Is hope limited to an anticipated reunion with loved ones in heaven and the glory of dwelling in the presence of God? That I look forward to. But with my dear husband and children and other loved ones here, I find it is difficult to feel excited about the severance of our soul intimacy and the suffering they will endure. I wonder what it really means to have hope. Hope for what? Longer life? Will just wanting it really make a difference?

I inwardly struggle. What good is hope if I die anyway? Is hope merely a feeling?

Questions such as these bark in my ear. They are unrelenting in their pursuit of my soul. They come from those mongrels that I call the hounds of hopelessness.

THE HOUNDS OF HOPELESSNESS

Though the exercises of my soul do strengthen and stretch me, I can be stopped dead in my tracks by the baying hounds of hopelessness. Even as I am learning more about the meaning of hope, if I am careless they will nip at my heels. They are real and fierce, never hesitating to sink their sharp teeth into my soul. I am learning that it is important both to recognize the sound of their howls and to run to the Source of hope.

THE HOUND OF FATIGUE

Our housing tract in the foothills of the San Bernardino mountains is often invaded by coyotes looking for food and water. We see them at night, wandering in pairs or alone, and more often hear their howls. They look so small and almost cute. It is easy to feel sorry for them. After all, we humans have taken over their land, and they are desperate for sustenance to survive. Realistically, these wild hounds are not as innocent as they appear. A few years ago my daughter's cat was attacked and beheaded on our front lawn.

The hound of fatigue is much like these benign-appearing coyotes. It invades our home, appearing unexpectedly.

"I will just rest and be refreshed and run from this creature," I say to myself.

But in crisis I am caught off guard and consumed by fatigue.

"I will paint. I will read and be restored," I have often told myself.

The hound of fatigue is stronger than my desire. My hands are numb. My eyes are blurred. My joints are prickling with flu-like pain.

The hound has cornered my soul, and I moan, "Maybe it's hopeless."

I am bored. I am too tired to think, and I sink teary-eyed to the floor.

THE HOUND OF DEPRESSION

Right on the heels of the hound of fatigue follows the howling hound of depression. It pushes me to a most vulnerable position, flat on my back. It pulls a gray shroud over my body, and I am hopelessly unable to throw it off.

I feel so "unspiritual" covered by this gray, and there are always a few who concur. "Real Christians don't wear gray!"

My soul moans, "I must be doomed. My life has been worthless. I have failed. My life is but a puff of anonymous gray. I'll probably be buried in gray."

The hound of depression stands guard, and I am immobile.

"Nothing changes, nothing will change," I mutter in an attempt to be honest and realistic. "How can I hope for something that is lost forever?"

Is it possible to escape these hounds and grasp again the brass ring of hope? Slowly I am learning how to recognize their howl. I tell Stuart, "I hear them. Help me to run!"

As I call out, I realize that I am powerless. I haven't the strength to be hopeful. As Job said:

> What strength do I have, that I should still hope?
> What prospects, that I should be patient?
> (Job 6:11)

> At least there is hope for a tree:
> If it is cut down, it will sprout again,
> and its new shoots will not fail.
> Its roots may grow old in the ground
> and its stump die in the soil,
> yet at the scent of water it will bud
> and put forth shoots like a plant.
> But man dies and is laid low;
> he breathes his last and is no more.
> As water disappears from the sea
> or a riverbed becomes parched and dry,
> so man lies down and does not rise;

till the heavens are no more, men will not awake
    or be roused from their sleep.
                         (Job 14:7–11)

If the only home I hope for is the grave,
    if I spread out my bed in darkness,
if I say to corruption, 'You are my father,'
    and to the worm, 'My mother' or 'My sister,'
where then is my hope?
    Who can see any hope for me?
Will it go down to the gates of death?
    Will we descend together into the dust?
                         (Job 17:13–16)

The hounds of hopelessness will not relent. They are not turned away by the sound of a cheerful voice. They are not intimidated by musings about the hereafter. The hounds of hopelessness are stopped only when they confront *power.*

I remember thinking about this for weeks after surgery. It was probably my lowest time. As well-wishers admonished me to have hope, I questioned what hope really means. I was skeptical about everyone's advice. After all, *they* were not feeling extreme fatigue, pumped full of drugs that make me feel like a vegetable, facing the death sentence.

The only answer I could glean from my well-wishers was that I could be content with the hope of eternal life in heaven. That is a glorious expectation. But when some would act as if I were "lucky," and they were the unfortunate ones to be dealing with this pagan world, I felt an emptiness in their wish.

As difficult as this time has been, I am not looking for an escape. As painful as it may get, I do not favor euthanasia. As marvelous as heaven will be, I am not eager to leave my husband and children. Only God knows the day and the hour that I will be called to my heavenly home, and until then I want to praise and proclaim His name on earth through relationships and work worthy of His name.

Therefore, I asked myself again and again, is there meaning to hope beyond the expectation of a future life? Is there a deeper meaning than the promise of a longer life on earth? What is the meaning of hope for me now, this day, this minute?

As if I had new ears, I listened to the voices in the world around me. I was struck by the meaninglessness of most magazines. They echoed the popular myth that hope is related to people connections, situation connections, rich connections.

PEOPLE CONNECTIONS

"Networking is essential for your future," they proclaim.

"You must know the right people. Business and social relationships are the key to success."

It is true that in our society we can move up the scale of power through our contacts with other people. That is not necessarily wrong; but it does not empower the soul. There is no connection between a busy social and business life and the measure of life in the soul.

CORRECT CONNECTIONS

Closely related to the myth of people connection is the myth that correct circumstances will empower my soul. With the correct clothes I am temporarily filled with hope; I feel accepted, connected. Perhaps, the media tells me, my soul feels empty because I have low self-esteem. Perhaps if I just lose weight or find the right hairdo, I will be filled with hope. These things are like cream puffs, filling the stomach but leaving my soul unnourished. They have nothing to do with my real-life crisis. They are immaterial, trivial.

RICH CONNECTIONS

Is it possible to feel satisfied and almost smugly spiritual when we are financially successful? On the one hand, I am accountable to God for the possessions He gives me. But on the other hand, I cannot credit my savings and investments to the enrichment of my soul. That is the myth of the get-rich leaders. After all, they say, money talks.

Am I lured into thinking that I would feel more hopeful if I could just pay off all my bills?

Hope for what? I ask myself. "When you set your eyes on it [riches], it is gone. For wealth certainly makes itself wings like an eagle that flies toward the heavens" (Proverbs 23:15 NASB).

In times like this, if I gained the whole world of riches but still lived with an empty soul, I would have nothing. How can my soul be filled with hope?

POWER CONNECTIONS

Hope is related to the measure of inner power, the power within my soul. When my situation is unchangeable, I feel hopeless, without power. My soul sags. When God fills my soul with hope, what is it that He does? I tried to analyze how this happened. What did people do or say that empowered my soul? What does God promise and do today to empower my soul?

In the larger arena of life, there is an obvious connection between power and hope. I was talking to my friend Mary Ellen, who lived abroad for several years with her husband and children. The country in which they lived was dominated politically by one party. Though the people voted for their leaders, they knew that their vote was worthless; the elections were a facade. Nothing would change. Stoicism and hopelessness were etched on the faces of the people. Without power there was no hope.

I thought about the women in our own country in past years who were not allowed to vote. When they were given the right to vote—if they took advantage of that right—their lives were changed. They were empowered. They had hope that they could make a difference.

When God empowers me, when my friends empower me to live this day, it is the deeper strengthening in my soul that gives me hope. It is a spiritual connection, satisfying to my soul, that gives me the surge of strength I need for daily living.

SOUL CONNECTION

The principle of soul connection shows us the real meaning of "hope."

The sixth principle. As I cling to the Source of soul power, I am able to regain vision and hope.

Soul connection is the action of holding onto and sharing the hope that empowers the soul. The day that I was reading in 1 Peter, I felt that I had found the first clue in the mystery of what hope means for my soul this moment.

> Praise be to the God and Father of our Lord Jesus Christ! In his great mercy he has given us new birth into a living hope through the resurrection of Jesus Christ from the dead,
>
> and into an inheritance that can never perish, spoil or fade—kept in heaven for you,
>
> who through faith are shielded by God's power until the coming of the salvation that is ready to be revealed in the last time.
>
> In this you greatly rejoice, though now for a little while you may have had to suffer grief in all kinds of trials.
>
> These have come so that your faith—of greater worth than gold, which perishes even though refined by fire—may be proved genuine and may result in praise, glory and honor when Jesus Christ is revealed. (1 Peter 1:3–7)

He has given us a living hope, a hope for this life, and an inheritance that can never perish, spoil, or fade. While my inheritance in heaven gives me the hope of anticipation, this living hope is also related to a Source of power for living this day.

Peter wrote that we are shielded by the power of God.

If I am not connecting with my realities and relationships today, but am living only in anticipation of my future hope in heaven, I cannot realize God's power in the present. God's promise of hope is not just a promise for *tomorrow*—so that somehow I can grit my teeth and tolerate today because there will be an escape tomorrow. I can also claim hope for today.

At the same time, I was reading in Ephesians and saw the following verses in a new light:

> I keep asking that the God of our Lord Jesus Christ, the glorious Father, may give you the Spirit of wisdom and revelation, so that you may know him better.
>
> I pray also that the eyes of your heart may be enlightened in order that you may know the hope to which he has called you, the riches of his glorious inheritance in the saints,
>
> and his incomparably great power for us who believe. That power is like the working of his mighty strength,

which he exerted in Christ when he raised him from the dead
and seated him at his right hand in the heavenly realms,

far above all rule and authority, power and dominion, and
every title that can be given, not only in the present age but also
in the one to come. (Ephesians 1:17–21)

As I know Him better, my eyes are enlightened. I see the richness of
the hope of my inheritance, and I also realize that He is not withholding
His incomparably great power from "us who believe." "For of His fullness
we have all received, and grace upon grace" (John 1:16 NASB).

His fullness "fills everything in every way" (Ephesians 1:23).

His power is available for me today to give me strength, grace, and joy
in living with my circumstances.

THE GOD CONNECTION

Who is this One whom I claim to be the source of my power and
hope? What is it that He actually does to give me hope? What is it that I
do to claim that hope? And what actually changes with hope? I want to
probe deeper and be practical. Since I am in this seemingly hopeless circumstance, this is very important to me.

WHO IS GOD?

Again, I look with new intensity at the character of God. Wouldn't
you investigate the character of someone who promised you hope? I look
closely and am reminded that He is love. He is faithful. He is righteous
and just. My soul opens and yearns for such a One, who has proven to be
a source of refuge and restoration to mankind.

> Your love, O Lord, reaches to the heavens,
>   your faithfulness to the skies.
> Your righteousness is like the mighty mountains,
>   your justice like the great deep.
> O Lord, you preserve both man and beast.
>   How priceless is your unfailing love!
> Both high and low among men
>   find refuge in the shadow of your wings.

They feast on the abundance of your house;
    you give them drink from your river of delights.
For with you is the fountain of life;
    in your light we see light.

                                  (Psalm 36:5–9)

WHAT DOES HE DO?

Is hope merely a feeling? I kept asking myself. *Am I expecting God to give me a feeling?* That is what I wanted—to feel good, to feel joy. I am beginning to learn that while joy is a *result* of hope, hope is deeper than a feeling. Hope is born in my soul by the infilling of His power. I looked at four ways that He empowers me.

God fills me with joy and peace. This is the result of His filling me, not something that I can grasp apart from Him. He not only fills me, but He is generous, so that I overflow with hope. "May the God of hope fill you with all joy and peace as you trust in him, so that you may overflow with hope by the power of the Holy Spirit" (Romans 15:13).

God promises future hope. "There is surely a future hope for you, and your hope will not be cut off" (Proverbs 23:18). What an encouragement to know that God specifically states in His Word that He will not cut off my hope. He is willing to continue filling me with hope.

God gives strength. He not only gives me enough to get through the day, but He empowers me to complete goals I never imagined—at the most unexpected times.

Do you not know?
    Have you not heard?
The Lord is the everlasting God,
    the Creator of the ends of the earth.
He will not grow tired or weary,
    and his understanding no one can fathom.
He gives strength to the weary
    and increases the power of the weak.
Even youths grow tired and weary,
    and young men stumble and fall;

but those who hope in the Lord
will renew their strength.
They will soar on wings like eagles;
they will run and not grow weary,
they will walk and not be faint.
(Isaiah 40:28–31)

God encourages me. His encouragement is eternal, and powerful, and secure. What a blessing to experience, by His grace, good hope and strength in every good deed and word.

May our Lord Jesus Christ himself and God our Father, who loved us and by his grace gave us eternal encouragement and good hope,
encourage your hearts and strengthen you in every good deed and word. (2 Thessalonians 2:16–17)

God did this so that, by two unchangeable things in which it is impossible for God to lie, we who have fled to take hold of the hope offered to us may be greatly encouraged.
We have this hope as an anchor for the soul, firm and secure. (Hebrews 6:18–19)

WHAT DO I DO?

This is where I exercise my soul connection with God. I am learning seven ways in which I exercise hope in Him.

I place hope in God. This indicates a deliberate action. I have a choice of where to place my hope. In my circumstances it is easier to pass up the lure of material things, but I am often drawn to put my hope in people in place of God. For example, my energy can go up and down, depending on what the doctor says. Am I seeking strength for today from a physical prognosis? I must put my hope in God for this day, and He will empower me.

May your unfailing love rest upon us, O Lord,
even as we put our hope in you.
(Psalm 33:22)

Why are you downcast, O my soul?
    Why so disturbed within me?
Put your hope in God, for I will yet praise him,
    my Savior and my God.

                    (Psalm 42:5)

I lift my soul to God by seeking His guidance and truth. My soul is too weak and worn to "feel" like seeking truth. Therefore, it is by a disciplined choice that I lift up my soul to God. I seek His guidance and truth because I know it is right for my soul.

To you, O Lord, I lift up my soul;
    in you I trust, O my God. . . .
No one whose hope is in you
    will ever be put to shame, . . .
Show me your ways, O Lord,
    teach me your paths;
guide me in your truth and teach me,
    for you are God my Savior,
    and my hope is in you all day long.
                (Psalm 25:1, 3, 4–5)

I rest in God alone. This is difficult for me—to rest. But I must be quiet. I must wait. I am learning to follow as "He makes me lie down in green pastures" and "leads me beside quiet waters," and there, "He restores my soul" (Psalm 23:2–3).

Find rest, O my soul, in God alone;
    my hope comes from him.
He alone is my rock and my salvation;
    he is my fortress, I will not be shaken.
                (Psalm 62:5–6)

I cling to God. Clinging means not letting go. I do not separate my soul into sacred and secular parts, but my whole soul clings to God day by day.

My soul clings to you;
    your right hand upholds me.
(Psalm 63:8)

I wait and search God's Word. How thankful I am for the Scriptures. The Old and New Testaments are far more than good books to read. They are God's living Word. As I search His Word, I am empowered by His Spirit.

I wait for the Lord, my soul waits,
    and in his word I put my hope.
My soul waits for the Lord
    more than watchmen wait for the morning,
    more than watchmen wait for the morning.
(Psalm 130:5–6)

For everything that was written in the past was written to teach us, so that through endurance and the encouragement of the Scriptures we might have hope. (Romans 15:4)

I seek wisdom from God. From the Scriptures and from the world around me, I keep learning, asking God for understanding and wisdom.

Know also that wisdom is sweet to your soul;
    if you find it, there is a future hope for you,
And your hope will not be cut off.
(Proverbs 24:14)

I rejoice in the glory of God. It is not in my weakness that I rejoice, but in the glory of God, which does not change because of my weakness. In the same way, it is not that I celebrate my pain, but that, even in pain, I rejoice in how God's love empowers me to persevere and grow.

We rejoice in the hope of the glory of God.
    Not only so, but we also rejoice in our sufferings, because we know that suffering produces perseverance;
    perseverance, character; and character, hope.

And hope does not disappoint us, because God has poured out his love into our hearts by the Holy Spirit, whom he has given us. (Romans 5:2–5)

WHAT DOES THIS CHANGE?

As God empowers me, my soul is settled with hope. It does not mean that I always have a great feeling, soaring above all troubles, but that I am not shaken. I am satisfied. I am strengthened and encouraged. I see a vast difference when I exercise soul connection with God and cling to Him for hope as opposed to the disconnected soul that strives for hope.

The soul that is striving for hope sees life's coincidences as part of godless synchronism. The soul that clings to God for hope recognizes life's "coincidences" as part of His sovereignty.

The soul that is striving for hope disciplines the mind to think positively through visualization. The soul that clings to God for hope recognizes that bringing positive thoughts into captivity is a process of divine transformation.

The soul that is striving for hope seeks to gain self-esteem. The soul that clings to God for hope is confident in the truth that it is redeemed.

The soul that is striving for hope is lured by the glitter of material riches. The soul that clings to God for hope is satisfied with a treasure of eternal riches.

The soul that is striving for hope determines a program for self-advancement. The soul that clings to God for hope discerns what is its divine purpose.

The soul that is striving for hope is set on keeping a strong will. The soul that clings to God for hope is set on following God's will.

The soul that is striving for hope is not opposed to using people. The soul that clings to God for hope grows in its understanding of people.

The soul that is striving for hope speaks of tolerance at every turn. The soul that clings to God for hope recognizes absolute values and worth.

The soul that is striving for hope seeks greatness as a source of power. The soul that clings to God for hope seeks grace as a source of power.

The soul that is striving for hope looks to status as the great connection. The soul that clings to God for hope knows that submission is the greatest connection.

CHOOSING TO MOVE BEYOND SURVIVAL

The source of hope for today and the future is an eternally connected relationship with God. John shows a beautiful picture of how I am related to Him through Jesus Christ, when he repeats the words of Jesus:

> I am the good shepherd. The good shepherd lays down his life for the sheep.
> The hired hand is not the shepherd who owns the sheep. So when he sees the wolf coming, he abandons the sheep and runs away. Then the wolf attacks the flock and scatters it.
> The man runs away because he is a hired hand and cares nothing for the sheep.
> I am the good shepherd; I know my sheep and my sheep know me—
> just as the Father knows me and I know the Father—and I lay down my life for the sheep.
> I have other sheep that are not of this sheep pen. I must bring them also. They too will listen to my voice, and there shall be one flock and one shepherd. (John 10:11–16)

He is the One who knows me best, who protects me, and speaks to me. He knows all my troubles. He knows my weaknesses, yet He loved me so much that He gave His life for me. He is the One who restores my soul. Psalm 23 illustrates numerous ways by which He fills me with hope. Can you identify them?

> The Lord is my shepherd, I shall not be in want.
>   He makes me lie down in green pastures,
> he leads me beside quiet waters,
>   he restores my soul.
> He guides me in paths of righteousness
>   for his name's sake.
> Even though I walk
>   through the valley of the shadow of death,

I will fear no evil,
>for you are with me;
your rod and your staff,
>they comfort me.
You prepare a table before me
>in the presence of my enemies;
You anoint my head with oil;
>my cup overflows.
Surely goodness and love will follow me
>all the days of my life,
and I will dwell in the house of the Lord forever.

SUMMARY

My goal in this exercise of soul connection is to hold on to hope. My desire is to confront hopelessness and regain vision and hope. Practical activities include accepting that God is the source of power for eternity and for this very moment. The benefit of this exercise is the encouragement of God's power and the experience of hope.

Chapter Seven

CONNECTING
with People and with God

As we come to the end of this writing, we admit we are only beginning to understand the mysteries of the soul. We continue to ask and explore questions. At the same time we see the world around us asking these questions: How do souls connect? And how does the soul connect with spirituality? We enter the discussion with some practical observations.

HOW DO SOULS CONNECT?

Stuart and I continue to feel the need for connection with other souls. There are still many unknowns. We are still in the midst. We do not know how long I will continue to need chemotherapy. We do not know if I will be treated at the City of Hope. We do not know if the cancer will go into remission.

It is the unknown and the uncontrollable that trigger panic in crisis. Facing the reality of this, I realize that though I have based my life on faith in God, I often "feel" more faith when I know and can control my circumstances.

This morning I awoke early and was praying silently as I lay under the covers. As I prayed, I was impressed with this recurring question from God: "Do you believe Me?"

I prayed for one family member and friend after another, yet I could hardly concentrate, for this question was repeated over and over: "Do you believe Me?"

Finally, I responded, "Yes, Lord. I believe You are Sovereign. Yes, I do believe You."

And that is truly the central issue. Do I believe He is who He says He is? Spiritual rituals and words (even the exercises in this book) are meaningless if I do not believe Him. And, if I do, the demonstration of my faith is trust.

If I believe He is sovereign, then I trust Him, even though I have no control and no certainty of healing.

If I believe He is love, then I trust Him, though I sometimes feel isolated and alone.

If I believe He is faithful, then I trust Him, though I cannot see what is happening.

If I believe He is just, then I trust Him, though I did not bring this cancer on myself.

If I believe He is righteous, then I trust Him, though everything seems all wrong.

I believe that God is sovereign.

One of the ways that God has demonstrated His sovereignty to us during this time has been through the timely encouragement of people. He has used multiple human relationships to lift us up, help us out, and give us guidance through these difficult days. Is this not a wonderful mystery—how others connect with us at just the right time, even when they do not know that a card, a call, a word, or a gift is needed most on the exact day it is received? We believe that God stirs the souls of human beings to reach out and connect with us at just the right time. We would like to leave you with some examples of the way He has used people to empower us and give us hope.

So many friends have said, "I don't know what to say."

We understand. Even with our present experience, we face the same loss for words when dealing with others' personal crises. We want everyone to know that even if your words were jumbled and you might have said something other than you intended, your effort, your empathy, your sincerity touched us.

We shall include here some practical examples of messages that have been meaningful to us, so that you may be encouraged to reach out. At first we wanted to mention the name of every one of you who have been so good to us, but the list was too long. Then, too, we realized we might easily make errors, and we would not want to leave anyone out. Therefore, we have tried to generally categorize the attitudes and actions that have been especially encouraging and empowering. Only in a few cases will the church leadership and some creative works be acknowledged by name.

EFFECTIVE ATTITUDES

We believe that God created us with the desire for human soul connection. It is part of His plan for filling our lives with daily hope. I have been overwhelmed with evidences of love and true caring from friends and family around the world. In the following, I have tried to analyze the characteristics of the human touch that are empowering.

Six qualities characterize the good deeds that effectively empower the soul. They are identified by a commitment to equality, timeliness, sensitivity, satisfaction, inspiration, and responsibility.

Equality means that we give without discrimination and with an attitude of respect. We are not condescending to the one who is ill or broken, even if as a result of sin. We give with an attitude of grace, treating others with dignity.

Timeliness means that we are not confined by convenient time or circumstances in our giving. We give our time as a gift without conditions. If the giver has to announce how inconvenienced he was or how rushed she feels, the goal of encouragement is lost.

Sensitivity means that we seek to understand the circumstances of the one we want to touch. We listen and learn rather than arrive with answers and instruction. After listening, we speak to appropriate concerns.

Satisfaction means that our words are nourishing and edifying. They may include helpful information, the sharing of experiences, and certainly biblical encouragement.

Inspiration means the sharing of a vision, gentle teaching, and leading. This may include ways in which God has led in your own life.

97

Responsibility means releasing the one in crisis to be as independent as possible. It means understanding the fine line between helping and making others dependent on you.

All of these qualities are inherent in good deeds that empower and encourage others.

EFFECTIVE ACTIONS

God has been gracious in sending friends with many practical encouragements during this time. I am amazed over and over again how faithful friends have given to me tokens of love and care during these long months. They have reached out with many good deeds.

At one point I was intrigued by the meaning of "good deeds," and what the biblical concept of good deeds is. Scripture is full of examples of what a good deed is and the value of doing good.

In brief, doing good is to be encouraged because:

1. It will glorify God (1 Peter 2:12).
2. It will silence ignorant talk (1 Peter 2:15).
3. It is commendable before God (1 Peter 2:20).
4. It enhances life (1 Peter 3:10–11).
5. It is from God (3 John 11).
6. It pleases God (Hebrews 13:16).
7. It is excellent and profitable (Titus 3:8).
8. It is the result of grace (Titus 2:11–14).
9. It sets an example (Titus 2:7–8).
10. It is noble (2 Timothy 2:20–21).
11. It is commanded (1 Timothy 6:18).
12. It is that for which we were created (Ephesians 2:8–9).
13. It will reap a harvest (Galatians 6:9–10).
14. It brings honor, glory, and peace (Romans 2:9–11).

As practical examples, we will mention here a number of the good deeds that others have done for us and coordinate them with Scriptures that tell of actions that are considered good deeds. These are grouped in twelve categories.

Doing God's will (Hebrews 13:16). We know that it is God's will for His children to pray, and we are deeply grateful for the hundreds of people who have told us that they are praying for us.

Do not hesitate to tell a person that you are praying for him or her. It is an encouragement to be prayed for by name. I will always be grateful for the way our friend and former pastor Dr. Larry Poland prays at the time a need is brought to him. He will often stop right there and ask to pray for that need at that moment. This practice has always been a blessing to me. The elders of our church came to our home and prayed with us. Our church women's ministry prays. Our small Koinonia groups pray. The Moody board of trustees called and prayed for me over the phone. Other friends have prayed with me over the telephone.

We are overwhelmed and grateful for God's grace in moving so many to pray. Still others have told me that they have awakened in the night and prayed for me. We believe that your prayers are effective whether we know about them or not. However, knowing is an additional encouragement.

Providing daily necessities (Titus 3:14). Making meals has been difficult for me during these months. It is often true in crisis, whether one is physically able or not, that mentally and emotionally one has difficulty planning and preparing for daily necessities. The women of our church, led by Donna Stark, have provided again in this area. Friends from other connections in life, work, and family have also brought meals and food gifts. Rides to and from medical appointments have been another great help. These good deeds lift the burden and encourage us.

Showing integrity in teaching (Titus 2:7–8). We are deeply grateful for the teaching and encouragement of our pastor Dr. Gary Inrig and his wife, Elizabeth. The consistency and integrity of their teaching have renewed our hope time and time again.

Demonstrating seriousness and soundness in speech (Titus 2:7–8). We are encouraged by those who call us and send literature about all types of cancer treatments. Both the information and the continuing calls to check on us demonstrate a seriousness of concern that bonds us to you. We also appreciate that you understand that we cannot always call back—and that you call us back instead.

Being generous, willing to share (1 Timothy 6:18). Gifts are an encouragement. We have enjoyed plants and flowers, candles, bath luxuries (soaps and gels), books, videotapes, and a few cuddly stuffed animals. It is good to remember that all reading material does not have to be about the subject of the crisis. It is helpful to read about other things. One dear friend of many years sends me copies of her weekly letter to her grandchildren. When she asked, I eagerly said I would like them. She has also allowed me to read a number of her writings of memories about teaching in the jails. Another creative friend gave me a basket full of powder, soaps, and lotions, with an appropriate verse attached to each one. Still another found a decorative basket of paper towels for my guest bathroom, a hygienic solution to the curbing of germs during my times of lowered immunity. The thoughtfulness and practicality of these gifts have given me joy and inspiration.

Bringing up children (1 Timothy 5:9–10). Though my children are grown, I am still greatly concerned about their lives and especially how this crisis is affecting them. Friends who pray for them, interact with them, and do good things for them give me hope and encouragement. The Lord has moved in the souls of so many to reach out in this way, and I am deeply grateful.

Showing hospitality (1 Timothy 5:9–10). Though my going out has been limited, we have treasured the times others have invited us to their homes or to a restaurant for a meal. The fellowship over the breaking of bread is like no other. Understanding the limitations of our situation, some friends have arranged to bring a meal and then stay to eat with us. That, too, has been a blessing.

Another example of help with hospitality occurred when our daughter Grace was married. A close friend organized all the housing for out-of-town guests. It was a wonderful gift of encouragement.

Washing the feet of the saints (1 Timothy 5:9–10). This may sound like a good deed from a different era, but someone close to me offered to give me a foot and hand massage. Believe me, it was wonderful. This is a sensitive and personal area, but under the right circumstances it is certainly a good deed.

Helping those in trouble (1 Timothy 5:9–10). Help has come in all forms. The first Christmas during this crisis, I could not find our Christmas stockings. A talented friend made beautiful stockings for each one of us. I remember the day when two friends from church were visiting and I was fretting about the dirty state of my house. Well, they just got up and started cleaning. One week, another friend paid for a housecleaner to come and help. My cousin from Colorado came to visit and helped organize the house to show for sale. I never thought I could accept such personal gestures and would never ask for them. But when they are given with the words "I'd like to do this for you," it is a great relief and encouragement.

Helping the poor (Acts 9:36). Though we are not in the category of poor, help with practical projects has saved us worry and extra expense. Two special men from the church have helped Stuart with several undertakings. One worked with him for several days on a painting project. Another, a contractor, sent his crew one day to inspect and fix some roof problems. Such help with things we probably would not do otherwise gave us great encouragement.

Making music in His name; singing praises to God (Psalms 92:1–2; 147:1). We have been loaned or given a few music videos and tapes. One family serenaded us. Music is a marvelous way to encourage the soul.

Praising the Lord; proclaiming His love and faithfulness (Psalm 92:1–2). Through phone calls, visits, cards, and letters, friends and family have empowered and encouraged us. Most include a direct, if not an indirect, indication of continuing prayer for us and praise for Him.

Phone calls are a definite encouragement. However, the desirability of calls may differ with each person and situation. The caregiver can be of great help in taking messages, but even he or she can become exhausted and unable to deal with a lengthy conversation. Just leaving a message on the answering machine can be encouraging.

Visits are in a similar category. Though I love to have visitors, some days I am just not physically up to it. It is helpful to receive a phone call ahead of time. On the other hand, I have had many days of feeling lonely and isolated when I wished someone would come. Some people have said, "Call me when you want me to come." That is difficult for one in crisis. It is overwhelming to plan and feel one must prepare for visitors. It is easier if friends take the initiative to call and simply ask, "Is this a good time?"

Sending cards and letters is one of the most significant ways to encourage friends in crisis. Written messages can be saved and reread. The graphics on cards can be admired for their beauty or humor. Each card reflects something of the personality of the sender and makes me feel embraced by their warmth. Sometimes the message on the card speaks for itself, but it is always good to add a few words of your own. This is where most people feel in a great dilemma. What should they write? There are no set right or wrong words. Sincerity is the best guide. However, for your encouragement, we include some of the remarks that people have written:

> "I love you and am praying for you."
>
> "With my love and concern."
>
> "I was so happy to see you."
>
> "Thanks for letting your old acquaintance know what you are struggling with so that we could pray for you."
>
> "We are continuing to remember you in prayer. You are special to us."
>
> "We were shocked and upset when you called and told us your news. Rest assured we will be praying for you and your family."
>
> "It's got to be a tough road you are traveling just now. Hang in there. We are praying for you each and every morning."
>
> "Just want you to know that all our thoughts and prayers are with you. We are available for anything we can do to help you."
>
> "I am praying for your health and stamina and just for all aspects of 'you.'"
>
> "Thinking of you and wanted to remind you of my love."

"Thought you might like to know that I lift your name up in prayer many times each day."

"Thinking of you today. Hopefully . . . Prayerfully . . . Thankfully . . . ."

"You are in my thoughts and prayers as you face a difficult and jarring situation. I trust the Lord is keeping you strong and secure in His love."

"Whatever I say won't be adequate and won't express my deep sorrow and concern. Just know that I love you, and that all the Segers [my maiden name] have meant so much to us these many years. You are often in my prayers. God is indeed a safe and comforting refuge. He gives more grace as our burdens become greater. As He meets every need moment by moment, knowing His presence strengthens and sustains even in the most difficult times. God's mercies are new every morning. Great is His faithfulness."

"I wish I could visit with you! Know that I'm praying for you and that I love you."

[To Stuart] "We are praying for strength and healing and peace for Miriam, and for encouragement and strength for you too in these trusting days. He is there; He will never leave you or forsake you."

"Just want to remind you of our love and prayers for you and yours."

"As you approach your surgery, I'm thinking about a profound statement a friend gave me recently . . . 'Peace isn't the absence of trouble, but the presence of adequate resources.'"

"You have been in my thoughts so much lately. I've been praying for you and your family daily and hope you are feeling uplifted by everyone's prayers. There are so many people who love you all so much, and we really miss you."

"I was so sorry to hear of your cancer. What a blow— even for a woman of strength and courage."

"I've been praying that every cancer cell is gone, that your healing will be rapid, and that pain will be minimal."

"We are so thankful to know the Lord is your refuge and strength, and that you are trusting Him."

A number of friends have shared their own experiences with pain and comfort. A beautiful example from my friend Carol follows. I received this early in December:

Dear Miriam,

You have been in my thoughts and prayers all week. I had hoped to see you this morning but didn't, so I thought I'd just drop you a note.

Over the past few years different parts of the Christmas story have been encouraging to me as I faced different situations.

I remember that when my dad passed away the thought that Jesus was my "Everlasting Father" was comforting. Last year as I was giving up my Education Director position and following what I feel was God's leading to take the job with parish nursing, I was very concerned that it might not turn out well and I would have burned the bridge of administration behind me. During that time, the message of Christmas—"Fear not"—was the most encouraging to me. It was like the Lord was telling me—"I will help you."

And He certainly has helped me in so many ways this year. I have known more physical pain this year than I have ever had in my life with my continuing knee problems—but also a very richness of His presence in the midst of the pain and opportunities for ministry.

I share these thoughts with you and my prayers that the Lord will be your Everlasting Father, Prince of Peace, and Mighty God in a real and special way this Christmas season.

Please let me know how I can be a support to you through these trying days.

Lovingly, Carol Frizzell

Ephesians 1:18, "I pray that the eyes of your heart may be enlightened, so that you will know—

—what is the hope of His calling

—the riches of the glory of His inheritance in the saints

—and the surpassing greatness of His power toward us who believe."

Carol's letter spoke to me so wonderfully because she revealed her own struggles and God's comfort in situations similar to mine. She knew that I had recently lost my dad; I was concerned about giving up teaching; I was experiencing pain. Her reference to the truths of the Christmas story were especially meaningful in the month of December.

Another friend also touched my emotions with poetry. Her original work, full of truth and understanding, was a great comfort.

ONCE AGAIN WE'LL SING
John 11:25–26

What can I say to you, my friend,
Whose hopes are shattered, dreams obscured?
I tell you, this is not the end.
There is a place where life secured
      To the heart of God begins anew;
      Its anchor sure in Christ alone,
      Alert to joys it never knew
      When it was all its own.
            There is a place of confidence
            Where nothing can extinguish light—
            The heart where dwells the uncommon sense
            Of Jesus' presence in the night.
Dear friend, I care; it's not I
Can take from you the pain you bear;
Just come with me, and we will cry
To Him who'll take our every care—
      And give to us Himself instead.
      The best of treasures ever had!
      He'll wipe away these tears we've shed,
      And make our mourning spirits glad.
            Hope of our lives, our Peace, our Light,
            Our resurrected Lord and King,
            Give to our earth-bound eyes Your sight,
            And once again we'll sing.

—Linda Mohler[1]

The most satisfying human soul connections are bonded by a spiritual connection, a connection that goes beyond professed mutual love for God. It is the deeper, awesome bond of His Spirit within us that draws us together. The power and mystery of His work in us intrigues the world and is causing a popular wave of interest in spirituality. From every walk of life, voices are responding to the question: How does the soul connect with spirituality?

HOW DOES THE SOUL CONNECT WITH SPIRITUALITY?

Even in the world of fashion design, manufacturers are trying to help us connect with "spirituality." Designers Dolce & Gabbana display likenesses of the Madonna and Child on skirts, tops, and dresses. Jean-Paul Gaultier includes nude Madonna images, crosses, hearts, and crowns of thorns. European designer Ann Demeulemeester prints the word "holy" on chic white garments. Angels are also popular as symbols on shirts, jewelry, and buttons.

Are these true connections to spirituality, or are these just another form of cultural acquiescence? Throughout the ages, many diametrically opposed belief systems have issued a claim on spirituality. From New Age to the occult, from scientism to supernaturalism, from Buddhism to naturalism, proponents of these creeds profess to be spiritual. A popular producer recently referred to his latest cinema production as a "spiritual experience." We hear simple statements from celebrities such as "I am becoming more spiritual."

The search for spirituality may be gaining popularity, but it is not new. Many years ago Isaiah asked:

> When men tell you to consult mediums and spiritists, who whisper and mutter, should not a people inquire of their God? Why consult the dead on behalf of the living?
>
> To the law and to the testimony! If they do not speak according to this word, they have no light of dawn.
>
> Distressed and hungry, they will roam through the land; when they are famished, they will become enraged and, looking upward, will curse their king and their God.

Then they will look toward the earth and see only distress and darkness and fearful gloom. and they will be thrust into utter darkness. (Isaiah 8:19–22)

The Word, the law, and the testimony are God's Word, the Bible. It is the only absolute and trustworthy standard for spirituality. Instead of searching the world for symbols of spirituality, we should be searching the Word for the Source of spirituality.

The world's concern with and ignorance of true spirituality is not exclusive to this age. Paul wrote:

I am astonished that you are so quickly deserting the one who called you by the grace of Christ and are turning to a different gospel—

which is really no gospel at all. Evidently some people are throwing you into confusion and are trying to pervert the gospel of Christ.

But even if we or an angel from heaven should preach a gospel other than the one we preached to you, let him be eternally condemned!

As we have already said, so now I say again: If anybody is preaching to you a gospel other than what you accepted, let him be eternally condemned! (Galatians 1:6–9)

What is the gospel, the good news, about spirituality? Is spirituality something I can achieve through some connection to principles in this world? Paul clarifies the situation once again:

So also, . . . we were in slavery under the basic principles of the world.

But when the time had fully come, God sent his Son, born of a woman, born under law,

to redeem those under law, that we might receive the full rights of sons.

Because you are sons, God sent the Spirit of his Son into our hearts, the Spirit who calls out, "Abba, Father." (Galatians 4:3–6)

So I say, live by the Spirit . . . . the sinful nature desires what is contrary to the Spirit, and the Spirit what is contrary to the sinful nature . . . . But the fruit of the Spirit is love, joy, peace, patience, kindness, goodness, faithfulness, gentleness and self-control . . . . Since we live by the Spirit, let us keep in step with the Spirit.

(Galatians 5:16, 17, 22–23, 25)

The Holy Spirit is the connection to true spirituality. The good news is that when we believe in God's Son, Jesus, we are "born of the Spirit" (John 3:8, 16). That is the moment when the soul connects with spirituality. And we are blessed by the evidence of the Holy Spirit as we discover love, joy, peace, patience, kindness, goodness, faithfulness, gentleness, and self-control growing in our souls.

It is our connection to true spirituality through the Holy Spirit that gives reality to our faith and life to our dreams, allowing us to praise the Lord who restores our soul.

> Praise the Lord, O my soul;
> all my inmost being, praise his holy name.
> Praise the Lord, O my soul,
> and forget not all his benefits—
> who forgives all your sins
> and heals all your diseases,
> who redeems your life from the pit
> and crowns you with love and compassion,
> who satisfies your desires with good things
> so that your youth is renewed like the eagle's.
> The Lord works righteousness
> and justice for all the oppressed.
> He made known his ways to Moses,
> his deeds to the people of Israel:
> The Lord is compassionate and gracious,
> slow to anger, abounding in love.
> He will not always accuse,
> nor will he harbor his anger forever;

he does not treat us as our sins deserve
    or repay us according to our iniquities.
For as high as the heavens are above the earth,
    so great is his love for those who fear him;
as far as the east is from the west,
    so far has he removed our transgressions from us.
As a father has compassion on his children,
    so the Lord has compassion on those who fear him;
for he knows how we are formed,
    he remembers that we are dust.
As for man, his days are like grass,
    he flourishes like a flower of the field;
the wind blows over it and it is gone,
    and its place remembers it no more.
But from everlasting to everlasting
    the Lord's love is with those who fear him,
    and his righteousness with their children's children—
with those who keep his covenant
    and remember to obey his precepts.
The Lord has established his throne in heaven,
    and his kingdom rules over all.
Praise the Lord, you his angels,
    you mighty ones who do his bidding,
    who obey his word.
Praise the Lord, all his heavenly hosts,
    you his servants who do his will.
Praise the Lord, all his works
    everywhere in his dominion.
Praise the Lord, O my soul.

                                     (Psalm 103)

EPILOGUE

STUART BUNDY

Throughout Miriam's extended battle with cancer, her constant theme was that the Big C be Christ, not cancer.

As she continually turned her soul toward Him, her soul was restored. Also, her great desire to better understand the attributes of God, so that she could worship Him even in her sickbed, restored her soul. As a result, she was able to think of others and their needs. While taking chemotherapy, she reviewed the prayer cards given by friends and prayed for them.

What she wrote in our book about the restoration of her soul was her personal experience, which was an example to all who knew her of God's grace in great times of need. So, when on June 26, 1998, she was "promoted to glory," carried there by angels, we sensed she had been only waiting to have her soul completely and fully restored, and we rejoiced with her.

GRACE BUNDY COSBY

As I was growing up, my mother encouraged me to use my mind, be creative, and love others without pretense. At home, work, and in the community, friends and acquaintances were impacted by her genuine care and inspired by her dreams.

This book was her last effort of creativity on this earth. Her desire was to stimulate the mind and stir the heart of the reader. She hoped the focus would not be solely on terminal illness but also on its connection to the human soul.

I am thankful for my mother's drive to reach others through her writing. I think she has inspired us all.

VALERIE BUNDY

The first thing you noticed about my mother was her love for everyone else. It was as if there was a circle around her, enveloping everyone who came in contact with her. The characteristic everyone noticed and what she emanated was love.

I remember my mother's prayer cards, which were a symbol of her love for others. Walking into a darkened, sanitized hospital room, I would see her sitting on the bed with a big stack of cards. Each one bore someone's name and prayer request, and she would lovingly pray for every friend.

As if that list weren't long enough, she asked others about their prayer requests—nurses, grocery-store clerks, endless faces and names I couldn't remember. In the midst of all that was going on in her life, it was natural for her to love them and listen to their problems and care for them. She had learned what it means to follow the commandment to love, for it flowed through all her life.

JON BUNDY

My mother never saw the publishing of this book. She did not want this book to be another book about the soul. She wanted it to be about her relationship with Christ and how she trusted Him through the difficult times. When she had cancer, she was always trying to reach out and help others. She was a great woman, and all who knew her were touched by her. I hope that this book helps others to relate to the ones that they love.

As her son, there is one point that I would like to express to you all. If there is anyone you love, don't hesitate to tell him that. Life is precious and is not worth taking for granted.

I love you, Mom.

Appendix

SOUL CONNECTION:
With God and with People

Stuart asks, When the psalmist cried out, "O my soul!" what did he mean by *soul?*

During America's Great Awakening, songwriters seemed to know, for many songs were written with the soul in mind. There were hymn writers who encouraged our souls to "awake"; those who cautioned our souls to "be still"; others who instructed us to "guard" our souls; and, always, the writers who rejoiced when it was "well" with their souls.

It seemed commonly understood that one's eternal soul was the individual *person,* with conscience, will, intelligence, emotions. In more recent times, talk of the soul has faded, and more attention is given to what we call our "psyche" and its needs—on the one hand, anxieties, loneliness, fear, despair, anger and alienation, neuroses and psychoses, depression and emptiness; and on the other hand, a yearning for personal fulfillment, success and approval, and a hunger for "spirituality."

NEW INTEREST IN THE SOUL

New conversations and ideas have arisen concerning the soul.

Thomas Moore writes in the Introduction to *Care of the Soul,* "When the soul is neglected, it does not just go away, it appears symptomatically in obsessions, addictions, violence and loss of meaning . . . we have lost our wisdom about the soul, even our interest in it."[1]

Along with Thomas Moore, a wide spectrum of society today speaks of new interest in theories of the soul both past and present. Three paths of thought are sometimes intertwined, causing ambiguity for those seeking meaning. There is the path of Carl Jung, the path of the New Age, and the path of the early church theologians.

THE PATH OF CARL JUNG

Leading the movement in popular literature and some academic circles are the contemporary followers of Carl Jung, who developed the theory of the "universal soul," of which he believed we are all a part. This he called our "collective unconscious." This view holds that we come in touch with that part of the universal soul that is our own by understanding the myths and traditions of the past.

For example, they would say, a Peruvian Indian today certainly has as a part of his soul the traditions and mythology of his ancestors, the Incas. He can thus better understand his own soul by understanding the past culture.

For Jung, it was not necessary to discover the origin of universal values. Rather, he accepted the existence of a universal love, a spirituality, and even the "dark side" of the universal soul. Jung and those who follow him have come to be known as "archetypal" psychologists and psychiatrists. An archetype is an original. It sets a pattern. In this case, definitive periods in history have defined archetypal souls, which set a pattern for the souls that follow and participate in the "collective unconscious." According to this thinking, each of us is developing our own individuality with elements of the archetypal soul.

THE PATH OF NEW AGE

Here the New Age movement has identified with Jungian thought. It too postulates the concept of a universal soul, of which it says we are all a part. A New Age advocate might exclaim, "By returning to Machu Picchu in the Peruvian mountains, I came in touch with my universal soul and the soul of the past that lives in me today."

Among the advocates of New Age are those who believe in reincarnation. They believe that the soul not only exists but at death will pass from the body to a new body. Some practice both communication with departed souls through channeling and the consultation of psychics, those who claim to know the activities of souls.

THE PATH OF THE EARLY CHURCH

We today are not the only ones who have had to define the origins and identity of the soul. Early in church history, theologians dealt actively with this very issue. Even then, some were arguing that the soul had a pre-existent state and the soul should struggle to regain its primitive form through contact with the "universal soul."

In Robert L. Wise's modern language translation of Augustine, the soul is seen as a gift from God. He translates:

> For heaven's sake don't let anyone persuade you that the soul partakes of the nature of God! To believe that the soul is a part of God is a terrible heresy. The worst heretics say that the soul emanated out of God . . . what you must say is that the soul comes from God as a gift, and gift alone.[2]

Wise further reveals Augustine's thinking in his contemporized statement about the soul's abilities: "The soul was endowed with reason and intelligence for dominion over the creation. As He formed us from the dust of the earth, God breathed the soul into existence."[3]

Even these brief glimpses of the archetypal soul, the universal and reincarnated soul, and the soul views of early church theology show us the confusion that can easily exist in defining the term *soul.* We hope to add some clarity to the meaning of soul through Scripture and the insights of contemporary Christian writers.

CONTEMPORARY INSIGHTS

Because we are part of a scientifically oriented society, attempting to dissect or observe every concept under the electronic microscope, the idea of a soul with its many attributes, and without clarity of design, is challenging. We have been taught by the scientific method to believe only what we can see, touch, taste, or hear. Furthermore, humans are extremely complex beings, and attempting to separate out parts of our being is like peeling the skin of an onion. If we peel all away, there is nothing, yet we know that a person still exists even after an intellectual peeling.

Though it is totally impossible to define with precision what the soul is, we know it is a gift from God to us, making each of us a unique individual with a free will. The soul is a mystery. In its totality, it is greater than the sum of its parts. However, to begin to have some understanding of what a great gift God has given us, we should attempt to have some understanding of attributes of the human soul.

Allen C. Guelzo comments on the attributes of sensations, thought episodes, decisions, and instances of belief as occurrences within the mind, and he adds, "That is not a bad way of accounting for the soul."[4]

CONSCIOUSNESS

Through all human history, man has become aware of different views, his consciousness of himself, and his consciousness of God.

Scripture pours forth the concept that human consciousness and God consciousness are part of the immortal soul that God breathed into each of us. Isaiah wrote, "I delight greatly in the Lord; my soul rejoices in my God. For he has clothed me with garments of salvation and arrayed me in a robe of righteousness" (Isaiah 61:10).

There can be no clearer statement of human consciousness in a direct relationship with God than David's statement, "To you, O Lord, I lift up my soul; in you I trust, O my God" (Psalm 25:1–2).

SENSATIONS

Mental perceptions of emotions and physical responses are both elements of sensations. Thus the psalmist said, "My soul is in anguish. . . . My soul thirsts for God . . . My soul is weary with sorrow" (Psalms 6:3; 42:2; 119:28).

This speaks of the depth of his sensations. It also depicts the range of his emotions and the gut-wrenching physical manifestations of his anguish.

In common parlance today, when people speak of the soul, they are often thinking of the emotional element of this multidimensional mystery. Oksana Baiul, the Olympics star, said that it helps to pour out tears and let loose laughter. "It shows you have a soul."⁵ Indeed, there is so much emphasis on the soul's *sensations* that it is tempting to believe that they are the totality of the soul. Yet this wondrous soul is much more.

THOUGHT EPISODES

An "episode" is an event that is separate and distinct and is capable of creating part of a larger whole. Our souls go beyond the mechanics of the brain. They are capable of creating thought events and then linking them with the larger whole. For example, we can understand a thought episode of the resurrection and relate it to the whole doctrine of personal salvation. One image of Christ on the cross brings to mind how He died for us and thereby brought us salvation.

Our souls are capable not only of understanding thought episodes but also of creating them. A composer can create a thought episode with each element of a musical score, the notes and the sounds from the violins to the tubas. Each thought episode will be part of a perfect whole, expressed as a beautiful symphony.

Is not this element of the human soul—the ability to produce thought episodes and link them to a greater whole—a most marvelous gift, which makes mankind a special creation of God, indeed?

DECISIONS

The decisions of life, those decisions that determine the very course of our lives, are a function of the soul, and our best decisions are based on thought episodes.

When the psalmist said, "My soul will boast in the Lord" (Psalm 34:2), he made a conscious decision in his soul as to whom he would give credit for his successes.

Conversely, Micah was speaking of the decision of the soul to sin when he wrote, "The sin of my soul" (Micah 6:7); and Ezekiel wrote, "The soul who sins . . . will die" (Ezekiel 18:4).

It is the human soul that determines its own destiny by the decisions that it makes in regard to its relationship to its Creator. This is truly a wondrous gift with eternal consequences.

INSTANCES OF BELIEF

The decisions of life bring those instances of belief that transform our lives. David cried out, "O Lord, . . . say to my soul, 'I am your salvation'" (Psalm 35:1, 3).

What a dramatic instance of belief as his soul responded, "My soul will rejoice in the Lord and delight in his salvation" (Psalm 35:9).

DEFINING ESSENCE

Very few people become aware of the depth of the soul until it is activated by crisis. Like an earthquake making us acutely aware of our resources or lack of them, crisis reveals what we have stored in our innermost being. This inner being—the immaterial part of me—is made in the image of God, capable of emotions, thought, decisions, and belief. This inner person is the soul.

While I struggle to grasp the manifestations of the soul that merge and interact as one, God through His Word discerns the areas of depth or shallowness within me. Therefore, as I store the Word of God within me, I am instantly alerted to the condition of my soul. "For the word of God is living and active. Sharper than any double-edged sword, it penetrates even to dividing soul and spirit, joints and marrow; it judges the thoughts and attitudes of the heart" (Hebrews 4:12).

At the same time, His Word is the key to restoring the resources of power, faith, and dreams within me.

> The law of the Lord is perfect,
> reviving the soul;
> The statutes of the Lord are trustworthy,
> making wise the simple.
> The precepts of the Lord are right,
> giving joy to the heart.
> The commands of the Lord are radiant,
> giving light to the eyes.
>
> (Psalm 19:7–8)

My soul can rejoice that it is designed and defined by God. I can come before Him without fear, for He already knows what is in the storehouse of my soul.

> Nothing in all creation is hidden from God's sight. Everything is uncovered and laid bare before the eyes of him to whom we must give account.
> Therefore, since we have a great high priest who has gone through the heavens, Jesus the Son of God . . .
> Let us then approach the throne of grace with confidence, so that we may receive mercy and find grace to help us in our time of need. (Hebrews 4:13–14,16)

> Praise the Lord, O my soul;
>> all my inmost being, praise his holy name.
>>> (Psalm 103:1)

NOTES

Chapter 1

1. Oswald Chambers, *My Utmost for His Highest* (Uhrichsville, Ohio: Barbour), Sept. 20 reading. This edition is published by special arrangement with and permission of Discovery House Publishers. Copyright 1991 by Discovery House Publishers.
2. For further definition see W.E. Vine, *Vine's Complete Expository Dictionary of Old and New Testament Words* (Nashville: Nelson, 1985), 222.

Chapter 7

1. Linda Mohler, 1984. Used by permission.

Appendix

1. Thomas Moore, *Care of the Soul* (New York: Harper Collins, 1994), xi.
2. Robert L. Wise, *Quest for the Soul* (Nashville: Thomas Nelson, 1996), 147–48.
3. Ibid., 147.
4. Allen C. Guelzo, "Soulless," *Books and Culture,* vol.4, no.1 (Jan./Feb. 1998), 23.
5. Interview of Oksana Baiul, *The Press-Enterprise Parade Magazine,* June 15, 1997, 24.